About the Author

Angela Norris is a former journalist. She grew up in Knott End, where her story is set. After newspapers, she worked as a health promotion specialist followed by various roles as a researcher, lecturer, project officer and community engagement officer. Now semi-retired, she has returned to her first love – writing.

Dancing to the Beat of the Tide

Growing Up by the Sea in the Sixties and Seventies

Angela Norris

Matador
9 Priory Business Park,
Wistow Road, Kibworth Beauchamp,
Leicestershire. LE8 0RX
Tel: 0116 279 2299
Email: books@troubador.co.uk
Web: www.troubador.co.uk/matador
Twitter: @matadorbooks

ISBN 978 1785899 690

British Library Cataloguing in Publication Data.
A catalogue record for this book is available from the British Library.

Printed and bound by CPI Group (UK) Ltd, Croydon, CR0 4YY
Typeset in 11pt Minion Pro by Troubador Publishing Ltd, Leicester, UK

Matador is an imprint of Troubador Publishing Ltd

This book is dedicated to
Keith

Introduction

They say everyone has a defining moment, and I can remember mine. It's 1975, a warm summer's afternoon and I'm floating along Liverpool's Dale Street dressed in a white cheesecloth blouse with a pink chiffon scarf artfully draped around my neck and blue bell-bottomed jeans, hair flicked back to the side in soft curls. Catching a glimpse of myself in a shop window, I look the embodiment of seventies cool: fresh-faced and just eighteen years old, ambling along with all the insouciance of youth. From inside a boutique, the haunting sounds of 10cc's 'I'm Not in Love' drift across the busy street thronged with shoppers, and there's a palpable sense of buoyancy in the air of this musical city.

There's a lightness in my step because I'm on my way back to Lime Street Station feeling demob happy after finishing the first year of my journalism training. Located a couple of streets away from Dale Street is the independent college of journalism which I've been attending on day release from my role as a junior reporter on The Garstang Courier, a small rural weekly newspaper. My job is one that seems to have been created just for me; it's thrilling and exciting and precarious – and a world away from my parents' aspirations for me to follow a 'safe' career in teaching.

And, contrary to what 10cc are singing, there is no disguising the fact that I *am* in love. I'm dewy-eyed and besotted with the boy of my dreams, flushed with the freshness of a young romance that's full of hope and promise, like a shimmering meadow on a spring morning.

Right then, at that moment, it felt as if destiny had handed me a present in its entire gift-wrapped gorgeousness. There I was: young; full of energy and optimism; on the threshold of my career, with the whole of my life stretched out lavishly in front of me. And as I walked along Dale Street that day, I distinctly remember thinking, life absolutely can't get any better than this.

My day-release course was one element of my training, but the real learning took place in a shabby little upstairs office in Church Street, Garstang, where The Courier was produced and turned out every Friday. My editor, Tom Dooley, would drum in to me that everybody had a story to tell.

'People are nosy,' he told me. 'They want to hear all about other people. It's what sells papers. Inside every person there is a story, somewhere. And it's your job to go and find it.'

As a roving cub reporter I was duly dispatched to circulate among the good citizens of Garstang and the rural villages in Over Wyre, and sniff out stories about people, a newshound in the making. Golden weddings, graduations, a vicar retiring, a teacher winning a coveted prize for beekeeping, or a WI member volunteering to teach cookery skills to children in remotest Africa – all counted as stories in Tom's journalistic rulebook.

With a rural newspaper like The Garstang Courier, 'hard news' – violent crimes, major disasters, political intrigue, the stuff of the national and regional newspapers – was in short supply. It meant we had to rely on human-interest stories to fill the paper: stories about other people's lives. It was a strategy that must have worked because people bought The Courier in droves week in, week out.

Now, coming to the end of my career, I've decided to write my story. I've had an exciting and diverse working life, moving from journalism to health promotion and, later, to community engagement and project work, with lecturing and research in between. But at heart, I've always been a journalist.

Embarking on one's memoirs might seem on the surface a terribly pretentious and self-indulgent thing to do. After all, I'm not a B-list celebrity, a politician or a minor sports star. I haven't trekked to the South Pole, or invented a device to stop cakes tasting scrumptious, or put men on the moon. I've lived what could typically be described as an ordinary life. And yet within that ordinary life, as my editor constantly reminded me, there lurks a story. My story.

At first, writing about my life was intended to be nothing more than a project for semi-retirement, something to occupy my time and fill the empty afternoons stretching out before full-blown retirement. My aim was to get something written down for my sons and grandchildren in the hope that they might see there is more to me than simply being their mum and grandma. Like many other people immersed in life-story writing, somewhat loftily, I wanted to create my own social history. The thinking behind this was that, if they want to delve into the family story, *Who Do You Think You Are?* style, I'll have given them a starting point.

But then it occurred to me that my memories might resonate with those who grew up at the same time as me. As anyone who lived through the sixties and seventies will testify, they were exciting times for pop music, film, fashion, and dance. I grew up cutting my teeth to the heady beat of the Beatles and the Dave Clark Five, and dousing the hormonal fires of adolescence to the tunes of Rod Stewart, T. Rex, and the like. As a teenager in the seventies, life for me was about dealing with the tribulations of the eleven-plus and surviving secondary modern school. It was about first romance, and career options, and listening to the sage advice of Cathy and Claire in *Jackie* magazine, and taking those teetering platform-soled steps towards adulthood. And it was about dancing – literally and metaphorically – through all of this.

My story is set in Knott End and Preesall – the villages of my birth, where I've lived for most of my life – located on the breezy Lancashire coastline, halfway or so between brash Blackpool and its more sedate sister, Morecambe. Within winking distance of Preesall lies its twin, Knott End-on-Sea, a coastal town overlooking Morecambe Bay. Knott End and Preesall are part of a rural hinterland known as the Over Wyre district, so called because of the location of the villages on the banks of the River Wyre, the narrow waterway separating Knott End from Fleetwood. Over Wyre born and bred, I can proudly proclaim myself to be a true 'sand grown 'un', as we're known locally, the blood of the River Wyre flowing through my veins.

Since my sixties childhood and seventies teenage years, I've witnessed a tidal wave of social change in the place of my birth. The green fields of childhood have disappeared, swallowed up by forests of purpose-built retirement bungalows. Like many sand grown 'uns, I've watched Knott End and Preesall segue from being two distinct small rural villages in to one amorphous small town. Shops, cafes and the Verona cinema – for many years part of the fabric of the local community – have long since disappeared, along with a way of life that in many ways seemed so much gentler, though of course it's easy to look back through the soft lenses of sentimentality.

And yet, despite all the changes, Knott End, like a stately old lady, retains her quiet and genteel beauty, with the sand and the sea and the tide as her beating heart, and the influx of newcomers breathing palpable new life and a sense of community in to her old bones. My own story is, in many ways, intertwined with the story of Knott End, Preesall, and Pilling where we later moved. For we have each danced against a broader backcloth of social and cultural change.

As one of the unexpected pleasures of researching my story, I've been able to renew old acquaintances. There's been lots of laughter, and lots of meetings over coffee or lunch – or, in the case of one former teacher, wine. Yes, writing my life story has been fun, despite the few painful memories that occasionally resurfaced. It has been a life-affirming ride, a voyage of self-discovery.

Some names have been changed out of respect for those who wish to remain anonymous, and also to protect the identity of those I haven't been able to track down for their permission.

1

'Baby, I Love You.'

In 1956, the Suez crisis was raging, Elvis Presley had a number-one hit with 'Heartbreak Hotel' and the government introduced Premium Bonds as an incentive to encourage families to save. It was also the year I took my first peek at the world; I was born in Blackpool Victoria Hospital on 12 November 1956, at three in the morning, weighing a little over seven pounds. I was a beautiful baby, by all accounts. My parents christened me Angela Dawn because they likened my arrival in to the world to that of an angel at dawn.

'You were a bonny little thing,' my mum used to tell me. 'A proper little Shirley Temple lookalike, with a mass of golden curls, big brown eyes, dimples, and a really placid nature.'

Then she would go and spoil it all by adding, 'Mind you, everything changed when you reached your teens, and your hormones kicked in.'

Not only was my birth a source of joy to my family but it was also greeted with great jubilation by our neighbours. I was the first baby to arrive on our row of houses on Elletson Terrace, in the grand-sounding Park Lane, for several years according to one of our neighbours, Marlene Cross, who lived down the road from us.

My parents were both twenty-three years old when they had me – young by today's standards. My dad worked as a master joiner with his dad – my grandad. They ran a small business from a workshop in nearby Pilling. Prior to her marriage, my mum had worked as a secretary but gave up her job when she had a family.

My mum, Norma – named after the thirties film star Norma Shearer – was slim and dainty with delicate features and porcelain-smooth, shiny skin. She had tiny feet and small hands. She wore her dark brown hair fashionably short and curly, and always dressed smartly, favouring pretty full-skirted dresses that enhanced her gentle femininity. Because of a congenital deformity, her fingers were bent and misshapen and her spine was slightly curved, a condition that became more pronounced as she grew older. She often used to say she was thankful none of her children had inherited her genetic blueprint.

My dad, Roy, at just over six feet tall, towered over Mum. He was, and still is, slim. Back in my childhood, he was rarely ever seen out of his regulation workwear: blue overalls with bib and braces, worn over a green-and-brown checked shirt, rolled up at the sleeves, and with a flat tweed cap atop his thick, dark wavy hair. Tucked behind his ears would be a yellow-and-black striped pencil or, sometimes, an unsmoked Woodbine and peeping out from the upper pockets of his overalls, a folded ruler. He wore his joiner's uniform with pride, for it spoke of his status as family breadwinner, and he was proud of his working-class roots.

My mum gave up her job as a secretary when I was born so that she could devote her life to motherhood and housewifely pursuits. There was nothing unusual about this; after all, it was the era of the fifties housewife.

'I didn't go out to work and I never wanted to,' she would often say to me. 'I always felt there was no one good enough to bring up my children.'

While my mum settled in to cosy domesticity, my dad strove to build up his joinery business, working long into the evening. My brother, Geoffrey Alan, was born two years after me on 22

October 1958. I don't remember anything about this new baby arriving in the home. I suspect that's because I was busy being looked after by my granny and grandad, who spoilt me rotten.

'You were none of you planned,' Mum told me, candidly. 'We didn't have such a thing as contraception then.' What she meant was that contraception wasn't as widely used as it is today, and pregnancy was more a matter of fate than of timing.

Number 19 Elletson Terrace, Preesall, my first home, was one of a row of neat terraced houses, each with its own envelope-sized front garden. I can't remember a lot about this house, but I recall we had two downstairs rooms: a living room which doubled up as a dining room, for every day use, and a lounge, a second living room reserved for Christmas and special occasions, and regarded as the 'best' room. At the back of the house, the kitchen was dominated by a huge cast-iron stove, above which hung a wooden washing rack, suspended from the ceiling and festooned with clothes drying in the heat rising from the oven. Upstairs there were two bedrooms and a bathroom. I seem to remember the bathroom wall having clinical white wall tiles and a black lino floor with an inlaid diamond design. At the back of the house was a larger garden with a rear gate that opened up on to the back street.

With no showers back then, certainly not in our neighbourhood, we had a bath once a week, usually on a Saturday night. On the other days we had to make do with a 'good wash.' This, in my mum's books, constituted a quick lick with a soapy flannel over the hands, face, neck and ears, arms and knees, a ritual that was performed each evening at the bathroom sink. We weren't mucky kids, but by today's fastidious standards we probably weren't very clean either. As we grew older, we were assigned responsibility for our own ablutions, with Mum inspecting our necks and arms for the telltale 'tidemark.' This was the name she gave to the streak of caked, ingrained dirt across the back of the neck or inside the forearms that was a sure sign of neglectful washing. It's perhaps an appropriate term given our close proximity to the sea where the daily incoming tide leaves its timeless mark on our sleepy shores.

Like many neighbourhoods up and down the country in the fifties, Park Lane was the kind of road where people took pride in their homes. There seemed to be a sort of competition among the housewives as to who could produce the shiniest, most pristine home. One of our neighbours, Mrs Douglas, was so meticulous about keeping her house spick and span, she undertook a daily ritual of scrubbing her front step until it shone like moonstone. She was typical of that army of fifties housewives who carved their own identity in domesticity.

Along with the rest of the nation, Preesall, and its near-neighbour Knott End, were basking in post-war recovery, and enjoying the sense of calm that had descended on the country after the tumultuous years of war and rationing. While it is true to say that the district remained largely unscathed by the bombings and destruction, it was by no means immune to the effects of the war. Over Wyre folk endured their share of rationing and hardship along with everyone else. Not only that, but the district opened its arms wide to the troops of evacuees who came flocking to the countryside from inner-city Manchester and Liverpool – many of them staying and making their home here after the war.

During the fifties, Knott End and Preesall had a combined population of around two thousand people, and it would be fair to say everyone knew each other. There's a familiar saying in this part of the world that goes, 'If you kick one person, you kick 'em all.' What it means is that most families were related to each other some way. Back then, with limited geographical mobility and fewer opportunities for social advancement, most families stayed put, as did their offspring who, more often than not, went on to marry someone within the community. These couples, in turn, procreated the next generation.

This led to an elaborate spider's web of intricate family networks, with tentacles of cousins and second cousins once removed – and probably some more unusual hybrids – being spun across the whole district. The Jenkinsons, the Holdens, and the Curwens were just some of the many local families who spawned generations of Over Wyre residents. As a result, not only did everyone know each other, it was quite possible they were related. You could find yourself at school sitting next to your cousin or second cousin-once-removed, and not even know it.

Back in the fifties, we didn't have much money, and my mum used to make our clothes with the help of a Singer sewing machine. She also had a knitting machine, an unwieldy contraption that had a sort of pulley device into which wool was threaded. There was a handle which you moved along, backwards and forwards, like a giant zip, and it made a zizzing sound as it went. In a trice, garments could be knocked up as if by magic, saving the need for the endless hours of knit, stitch and purl. Thanks to the knitting machine, we had a wardrobe of jumpers and cardigans in an assortment of rainbow colours.

Dad grew vegetables on his allotment and worked part-time as a fireman to earn extra money. He was a member of Preesall Fire Brigade, a motley crew of about a dozen men (no women: these were the days when firefighting was seen as 'men's work') whose main duties revolved around putting out chimney fires and heaving recalcitrant cows out of ditches. One of my earliest memories is of seeing Dad race down our back street in a state of semi-undress in response to the wailing of the fire siren summoning him to the station. Naturally, this was in the days before mobile phones and the internet, so when the fire siren sounded the whole community was on high alert.

The majority of homes were fuelled by coal fires, which meant chimney fires were common. They were usually caused by a rogue spark from the grate escaping up the chimney and coming into contact with compacted tar lining the chimney walls. This could generate a spectacular firework of flaming tar particles, which came spewing out of the chimney, accompanied by a thick pall of industrial black smoke, causing a sooty fog to descend on the neighbourhood. Washing that had been hung out to dry would be blackened, much to the chagrin of the housewives who were left with little option but to clean the whole lot again.

On one occasion my dad was working away from the house somewhere when the siren sounded. He raced to the fire station to be greeted by news of a chimney fire. As the fire engine sped away, he quickly discovered its destination – a house in Elletson Terrace: 19 Elletson Terrace, to be precise. His own home! I would have been four or five at the time. I can remember our house being besieged by a dozen or so firemen armed with acres of hose.

My mum was in hot water. Cleaning up in the aftermath of a chimney fire could be a mammoth task. Walls, curtains and furniture would be covered in a fine layer of soot that seemed to find every nook and cranny, and there was a lingering smell of smoke in every room. Depending on how zealous the firemen were with the hosepipe, there was also a fair chance of a watery mess surrounding the hearth and fireplace. Fortunately, in our case, the smoke damage was superficial, though it was still enough to cause my mum vexation as she ploughed her way through a major clean-up operation.

As for Dad, he was teased mercilessly by his colleagues for going to such extreme lengths to ensure he got paid extra money. Firefighters were paid for each call-out, so Dad was ribbed for having the gall to muster up a chimney fire at his own home just so he could claim some extra cash!

As a child, I'd play in the back street with the other children from the neighbourhood. It was a loose-gravelled street, relatively free of cars and a safe haven for play – save for the gravel which played havoc with your knees if you happened to fall, which we frequently did either from our tricycles or from chasing each other around. At this stage, we weren't yet old enough for 'big' bicycles.

For my fourth birthday, my dad made me a Wendy house. On the morning of my birthday, Mum told me to go to my bedroom window and look out, and there would be a surprise waiting for me. There, outside in the back garden, was Dad proudly standing next to the biggest Wendy house you've ever seen – at five feet high, with its own felted roof, linoleum-tiled floor and lilac-painted walls, it was every little girl's delight; a house just like the ones grown-ups had.

I spent many happy hours playing in my Wendy house with my favourite dolls, often joined by my friend Kay, whose father was the local police constable. They lived just down the road from us at the local police house, situated at the end of our row.

One day, playing in my Wendy house turned to high drama after Kay accidentally trapped my fingers in the door. The pain in my middle finger was excruciating. I howled even more when I realised a tiny flap of skin from the delicate tip of my finger was missing. My mum had to rush me to the doctor's. I still bear the scar to this day, a reminder of the local doctor's botched attempt to patch up the wound.

My parents started to notice I was walking with an awkward gait and appeared to be flat-footed and knock-kneed. After I was referred to Blackpool Victoria Hospital for tests, my parents' suspicions were confirmed: I had a congenital deformity which meant my legs, from the knee downward, were out of alignment. To correct it, I was ordered to wear special leg splints every evening while asleep.

They were ungainly devices. My mum had to strap a splint around each leg so that the area from knee to heel was encased in a canvas sleeve with adjustable metal straps. Fastening them on was a wrestling match each evening, for I hated wearing them.

I'd kick my legs in the air in protest as my mum valiantly battled to keep me still while she tried to secure the wretched things in place. Many was the morning she'd come in to my bedroom to find me blissfully asleep, leg splints tossed to the side of the bed like prosthetic limbs, having been yanked off by me some time during the night.

But somehow her persistence paid off. My mum christened the splints my 'fairy legs', promising me they would help my legs to get better and stronger. Her words turned out to be pearls of wisdom, for my legs are probably my best asset. Nowadays, of course, problems with flat-footedness and fallen arches are easily remedied with heel supports, and I suspect 'fairy legs' are a thing of the past.

As a child, Sunday school played a big part of my life. I started going to St Oswald's Sunday school before I'd begun primary school. The highlight of each year was the annual trip, visiting places such as Trentham Gardens in Staffordshire, Southport, or New Brighton. One year we went to Heysham Head, in those days a popular amusement park and tourist attraction. As we played on the adventure playground, I can distinctly remember hearing 'Telstar' by the Tornados blasting out from the loudspeakers. The record was named after the Telstar communications satellite, launched into orbit in July 1962, bringing with it the promise of a golden future in space-age discovery. I made a discovery of my own that day as I tried to pluck up the courage to go down a giant slide: I was afraid of both heights and fairgrounds, a dual fear that has stayed with me to this day.

One day, during Sunday school classes, we were asked to draw a picture of Jesus and his Apostles but, for some reason, I decided to draw a picture of the Beatles instead. It was the dawn of a new pop era and the Beatles were everywhere. Turn on the television and there were scenes of hordes of screaming fans waiting at the airport, anxious for a glimpse of the grinning foursome as they boarded a plane for America. On transistor radios 'She loves you' blared out with regularity. So who could blame me for wanting to worship the Beatles, instead of Jesus?

This was the time of the swinging sixties and there was a real sense of vibrancy. Music seemed to be everywhere: on the television, on the radio and on everyone's lips, for it was an era of sing your heart out. 'Glad all over' sang the Dave Clark Five, with the eponymous Dave Clark, good-looking with dark hair and a toothsome smile, grinning away as he blasted his drums. And it was so infectious; you had to hum along.

There were television programmes devoted to pop music, such as *Juke Box Jury* with the suave David Jacobs presiding over a panel of celebrity jurors who listened to newly released songs on a jukebox and were asked to vote on whether the records would be a 'hit' or a 'miss.' *Ready, Steady, Go!* aired on Friday evenings and was presented by Cathy McGowan whose miniskirts, long heavily fringed hairstyle and thick black eye make-up epitomised the sixties girl. I can remember Cathy as a smiley teenager, the sort you would love to have as your big sister.

Though only young, I can remember being caught up in the fervour of it all. Who could forget the American girl group The Ronettes with their big beehive hairdos, false eyelashes, spangly dresses, and dramatic songs 'Be My Baby' and 'Baby, I love You' belted out to a distinctive backing orchestra and vocals?

My mum, who was a huge Ronettes fan, decided to dress me up as a Ronette for Preesall's annual gala day. She created a beehive hairdo from a nest of black wool and plastered black eyeliner on my eyes, much to my dad's chagrin, for he hated make-up.

'What do you want to go out caked in that muck for?' he muttered. But Mum was a skilful tactician when it came to making him see reason.

'It'll rinse off easily enough,' she said. 'Just let her be a

Ronette for a few hours – it's not as if she's going to look like this forever.'

A turquoise jumpsuit completed the outfit, and I was duly ready for the fancy dress procession: a Ronette in miniature, though a world away from the famed American soul sisters. I would have been about five years old at the time. I can remember feeling as proud as punch as I walked along the streets of Preesall in my turquoise jumpsuit to the cheers of the waiting crowds.

Across the road from our house, tucked away among the trees and fronted by fields and a sweeping driveway, was stately Parrox Hall, home to the local squire Daniel Hope Elletson and his family. Once a year or so, Squire Elletson would host garden parties and fetes on his expansive lawns with an open invitation for local folk to attend. Scores of our neighbours would troop in through the opulent gates, anxious to peek into this privileged world.

Alongside the usual stalls and sideshows – tombola, ice cream, cakes, pin the tail on the donkey, and guess the name of a giant teddy bear – was the popular bran tub. As a small child, I can remember plunging my hands in to the soft sawdust to fish out a prize. Wrapped in brown paper was a peach-coloured notebook. I was delighted with this find, turning it over in my hands, pressing its cold plastic surface under my nose and inhaling the delicate, yet unmistakable, scent of crisp new paper inside. I couldn't wait to get home to practise drawing animal pictures and scribbling my name. Though I was only young and barely able to write, beyond the usual childlike scrawl, I like to think of this little notebook as my talisman for the career I was eventually to take – as a reporter recording people's lives.

2

A Tale of Two Grandmothers

As I grew up, both sets of grandparents were a huge influence on my life. My paternal grandparents, Granny and Grandad France, lived a hopscotch jump down the road from us in an end-of-terrace house in Parrox View. My maternal grandparents, Grandma and Grandad Bill, resided a twenty-minute walk away, in Lancaster Road.

My grandmothers were as different as chalk and cheese. Granny France, my paternal grandmother, was a formidable figure: big, bossy and domineering, but with a heart of buttery gold. She was a homemaker who prided herself on her role as queen of her kitchen.

In contrast, Grandma, my mum's mother, was literary-minded and saw herself as an aspiring writer. She regularly penned letters to the local newspaper, *The West Lancashire Evening Gazette*, which later became *The Evening Gazette*. Grandad Bill was a leading light on Preesall Urban District Council, later to become Preesall Town Council, and, as the wife of a local councillor, Grandma basked in the reflected glory of his position. She saw this as giving her status and credibility to write with some degree of authority about local affairs.

I think I am probably a curious amalgam of both my grandmothers, inheriting traits from each. I've gained some of my grandma's whimsical, ethereal qualities, and her love of literature and creativity. But I've also got my granny's earthy pragmatism, her strong will and iron determination.

Grandma hailed from Padiham, Burnley, one of eight siblings from a poor, working-class family. She often told the story of how, as a young woman, she'd been denied the opportunity to 'better herself' by her mean-spirited mother. At school, Grandma was a bright pupil and her teacher, spotting her potential, recommended her for entrance exams to technical college. At thirteen she passed the exams, and after leaving school she started her college course. This would have been a golden opportunity to broaden her education, and a passport to a life away from the relentless monotony and grime of the cotton mill.

But shortly after starting college, Grandma was ordered to leave by her mother who insisted on her going to work in the mill to bring in a wage. Grandma always profoundly regretted being denied the opportunity to 'make something of herself.' It was a source of frustration to her even after she'd married and had children. And it led to her seeking refuge in films and books to escape the drudgery of her life as a fifties housewife. My Auntie June – my mum's younger sister – remembers, as a child, travelling on the bus to Blackpool with Grandma to see the latest Hollywood offerings at the cinema. Sometimes they would go twice in one day, morning and afternoon, to view the latest films.

'She lived her life through books and films,' recalls June. 'It was almost as if she was trying to escape into a world of romance. She couldn't get enough of the cinema – weepy films, anything with Bette Davis and Clark Gable or Robert Mitchum – she just used to immerse herself. "It's not real," she'd say to me as I sat there crying. Afterwards we'd sometimes stay out for tea, and then go home on the bus.'

Grandma was a victim of her time, in an era when women were defined by their role as mothers and housewives, just as my own mother was when she had me in the fifties. Had she been born half a century or more later, I've no doubt she would have been a teacher, or even a journalist, or perhaps an actress, given her flamboyance and love of the stage (she was a member of Preesall WI Amateur Dramatics Society, as was my granny). As it was, she took a course in hairdressing and ran a small-scale hairdressing business, mainly for family and friends, from an upstairs bedroom at her home. She was always well groomed and her own immaculately coiffed dark hair was testimony to her skills: never a hair out of place. Her home was littered with knick-knacks and ornaments, and her bookshelves bulged with classic works of fiction.

She eventually found status of a kind when she became Mayoress of Preesall, accompanying Grandad Bill, in his mayoral duties, to civic functions. There are photographs of Grandma regally attired – in lavish, satin ballgown and tiara, with her mayoress's chain draped round her neck like glistening jewels, her hair immaculate – and looking suitably proud and stately. She'd come a long way from her mill-town origins and two-up two-down end-of-terrace home. But she was kind; she never forgot her roots, and she would regularly open her home and her heart to an army of nephews and nieces who holidayed in Preesall to escape the dreariness of Padiham.

If Grandma was a reluctant housewife, Granny was her antithesis, for she revelled in her role and identity as a housewife. She was the fifties housewife personified: a legend in her kitchen and a true homemaker who would bustle around cooking and baking, knitting and sewing, washing and ironing, and cleaning. She worked to a timetable, planned with military precision. Monday was washing day. Clothes would be washed by twin-tub (no automatic washing machines then) before being hung out to dry, and ironed later on the same day. Tuesday was cleaning day and Thursday was designated as baking day.

In between all of this, there would be bookkeeping (Granny

managed the administration for Grandad and Dad's joinery business) as well as knitting, sewing and darning – not to mention shopping, which meant daily treks to the shops in Knott End, a mile away. Granny regarded her walks to the shops as a valuable form of exercise and chance to meet with other like-minded housewives.

'What do you need to go to exercise classes for?' Granny used to ask me in almost accusatory tones when, many years later as a young mum, I became hooked on aerobics, a fetching sight in my lime-green leotard. 'I used to get all the exercise I needed doing housework and going shopping. That was enough to keep me fit.'

Back in my childhood, we used to go to Granny's regularly for meals, and there was always a sense of ritual attached to the preparation and serving of food. Mealtimes were accorded a sense of occasion; there were no TV meals, certainly not in my family.

Lunch – or dinner as it was known in our family – was served promptly at noon. This was the main meal of the day and it usually consisted of meat, or occasionally fish, and two veg, followed by pudding. As part of the ritual, my brother or I would be required to set the table. This meant laying a crisp white tablecloth, table mats and cutlery in an orderly manner to give the meal the sense of occasion it richly deserved.

Granny would sweep in carrying plates laden with thick slabs of roast beef swimming in rich, fatty gravy, accompanied by huge mountains of buttery mashed potatoes, heavily salted carrots and limp, watery cabbage, and watch us, hawk-eyed, as we climbed our way through the culinary equivalent of Mount Everest.

Leaving food was not an option. Granny would look crestfallen at the slice of beef lying forlornly at the side of the plate, and ask plaintively, 'Did you not like it, then? Well, what was wrong with it?' Feeling guilty, we would force the offending item down, nearly choking as we did so, in an attempt to placate her. Over time, we learnt that it was easier to eat everything that was put in front of us rather than risk Granny's chagrin, though a clean plate was inevitably taken as a signal for second helpings. Brandishing a serving spoon, she would plonk a dollop of mashed potato on the plate before we had chance to raise our hands in objection.

There was never any respite between courses. Once the first course was cleared, the plates were stacked away, ready for washing-up. Then it was time to dish up pudding. Granny's puddings were legendary. Rice pudding, sago pudding, tapioca pudding; all variants of a milk-and-grain concoction. Making them was simple; you sprinkled grain in an ovenproof dish, added copious amounts of sugar and milk, and baked until all the ingredients were absorbed. Granny's sago pudding was a sickly-sweet, rich, resinous mass that, once ingested, rested as heavy as a *Bible* in the stomach for hours.

Perhaps not surprisingly, after lunch we were quite literally stuffed, too full of food to do anything. Granny insisted on the dishes being washed – she always washed, clattering cups and plates down on the draining board with speed and gusto, and we wiped – before we did anything else. Once all the pots and pans had been neatly stacked away, she would declare, 'It's time for a nod,' whereupon we would all collapse into one of her comfortable armchairs and doze away the afternoon by the dying embers of the fire.

Granny was of the make-do-and-mend generation, and was adept at making a little go a long way. As befitted her wartime upbringing, she never wasted a scrap. Apples, plums, rhubarb and damsons would be whipped into delicious pies and jams. Chicken carcasses, vegetable peelings, eggshells and assorted leftovers would be popped into a pan and transformed into a tasty stock for soup. Socks would be darned until they looked like new.

She loved baking, and scones were her speciality – deliciously crisp on the outside and melt-in-the-mouth soft and buttery on the inside. To this day, I've never tasted a scone as good as the ones Granny made. I can still remember the aroma of her freshly baked scones, lifted out of the oven with the care and love accorded to new babies.

Teatimes were a quieter affair. Sated by too much food at lunch – or dinner, as it was known in our household – we would be offered a simple salad of cooked meats, salmon or cheese for tea, followed by the obligatory cakes or scones, served with lashings of butter. Granny reigned in the kitchen long before high cholesterol was heard of, yet she lived until the ripe and robust age of ninety-four, her arteries seemingly unaffected by her dietary excess.

If ordinary mealtimes were an occasion, then Christmas dinner was a culinary tour de force. In cooking Christmas dinner for a battalion of family members, Granny had a rival who vied with her for supremacy in the kitchen. This was Auntie Lizzie, her sister and cook-in-arms, who had professional experience in running a cafe. Between the two of them, they would draw up the battle lines, arguing over who carved the turkey and who made the bread sauce. Eventually these issues were resolved, and the result was an unfailingly glorious feast, cooked and served with military precision – succulent roast turkey, glistening carrots and Brussel sprouts, a lake of bread sauce, and all the other trimmings, all ready to be served at twelve o'clock prompt.

After we'd all finished the last spoonfuls of Christmas pudding swimming in brandy sauce, both Granny and Auntie Lizzie would positively glow from the praise offered by the appreciative gathering. Everyone would help clear away the dishes before collapsing into a chair to watch the Queen's speech and sleep away the festivities.

As I grew older, Granny taught me to cook and she taught me to be thrifty. From her, I learnt how to make toad-in-the hole, kedgeree and shepherd's pie, but I could never make scones the way she could. I almost always eat everything that's put in front of me, conditioned as I have been to respect food. Above all, Granny taught me that food provides emotional nourishment, especially when served up with a huge dollop of love.

It is true Granny didn't have the labour-saving devices we have: dishwashers, automatic washing machines, microwaves, high-tech food processors and bread makers. And I doubt very much whether she would have wanted them either; they would have removed some of the value of the work associated with housework. For her, the boundaries of life stopped at home, family and membership of Preesall WI – and she was happy and fulfilled in this role. Her floral-patterned nylon pinny was her uniform, her badge of identity.

There was never a speck of dust to be found anywhere, and she knew exactly where everything was kept. She taught me the value of things, and how to cook and bake, knit and sew; practical skills that have stood me in good stead, though I think she would cringe in heaven at my present-day efforts at needlecraft.

Granny and Grandad were hands-on grandparents and it was always a real treat to sleep overnight, when we'd be allowed to stay up a bit and watch television. We'd enjoy endless hours playing board games by the roaring fire in the living room – ludo, snakes and ladders, tiddlywinks and, when we were a bit older, Monopoly. We also played dominoes and snap.

In contrast to Granny, Grandad was a quieter, placid character, who would do anything for a peaceful life. Grandad bred bantams and I had one of my own, which I called Angela Bantam. She was a gentle creature who allowed me to push her around the garden in my doll's pram, quite unperturbed by my fussing.

Grandad smoked a pipe. One day I set fire to his hair. It happened as I was sitting on his knee, playing hairdressers. Just as I'd combed his thick mane of Brylcreemed hair down his face to give him a floppy Beatles-style fringe, an oily black tendril caught his pipe. His hair became engulfed in a swirl of flame. I screamed to Granny, who was in the kitchen. She came into the living room, took one look and dashed back to the kitchen to grab a damp tea towel in order to douse the flames. Needless to say, Grandad never allowed me to play hairdressers with his hair again!

Visits to my other grandparents, Grandma and Grandad Bill, were memorable for different reasons. Their home, Red Roofs in Lancaster Road, was a lovely detached house set in its own grounds, fronted by a rose garden. But appearances could be deceptive, for at the rear of the house Grandad Bill dealt in death, operating a gruesome poultry-dressing business, butchering chickens.

As we played outside, it was hard to avoid the pageant of horror fantasy that was being acted out in front of our eyes: decapitated hens being unceremoniously defeathered in a plucking machine, and ritually disembowelled, their slithery innards dumped inside a slop bin. As the final indignity, plumped and primped and skin shining as smoothly as a baby's bottom, the birds were strung up by their feet, heads downwards, and displayed like trophies, left to dry in their fly-infested prison. There was no way of disguising the sickly cloying stench of death.

Though Grandad Bill was the executioner in this macabre production line, (thankfully I never actually saw him kill any of the hens), it was all in a day's work to him. Home-grown poultry-dressing practices such as this – now a thing of the past thanks to stringent health and safety legislation and newer mass-production methods – were part of the fabric of rural life. As a blunt, straight-talking Yorkshireman, Grandad Bill never tried to shield us from the grim realities of his role.

'Don't fret, lass,' he would say, in response to my look of horror. 'How else can I put food on the table?'

My childhood experiences of poultry-dressing were a world away from the sanitised version of farming presented to today's youngsters through the array of vacuum-packed chicken gleaming in cellophane wrappings from the refrigerator compartments of the supermarkets. For it's probably true to say that children today are shielded from some of the harsher realities of farming in ways that my generation patently weren't. Later Grandad Bill's chickens would be delivered to the markets of Blackpool and Fleetwood to be purchased by eager customers.

At lunch time, Grandma would nearly always serve up platefuls of fat chips and thick slices of home-slaughtered, home-cooked plump, moist chicken breast on large oval glass dinner plates. Having observed the horrors of slaughter, it was almost too much to bear to be compelled to eat these sacrificial offerings. I can remember retching as I forcibly tried to swallow the chicken meat in order to please Grandma. To this day, I have never been able to eat chicken, no matter how artfully it is disguised.

3

The School on the Hill

I was nearly five when I started Preesall Fleetwood Charity School – known affectionately as Preesall High School because of its location on an elevated piece of land known locally as Preesall Hill - in 1961. I was following in the footsteps of my dad, who had been a pupil there from 1938 until leaving at the age of fifteen. During my dad's generation it wasn't uncommon to receive all your education, primary and secondary, at one school.

I don't remember much about my first day at school, other than that my teacher was Mrs Nickson and the head teacher was Mr Millward, a sharp-faced, thin-lipped man, with a deep Welsh accent. My mum said I was a sweet child with a disarming smile, and I knew how to use my charm with others, especially boys. She remembered how I used to smile winsomely, feigning helplessness when I felt I couldn't do something. Tying my shoelaces was a case in point. A boy in my class, Bill Taylor, would duly tie them for me, and then offer to walk home with me. I suppose you could say, at the tender age of five, he was my first 'boyfriend.' His acts of kindness must have stood him in good stead, for he eventually rose to become a senior ranking clergyman within the Church of England, working alongside the Archbishop of Canterbury.

After a year or so in Mrs Nickson's class, I moved up to Mrs Whitehead's class. She had reddish hair, wore glasses, was old

– well, to my six-year-old eyes she was old, as indeed were all teachers – and sharp-tongued. By all accounts, I was a quiet pupil who worked hard. At least that's what my school report said. In July 1964 I was awarded top marks for reading and spelling, and eight out of ten for arithmetic. However, I fared less well in history and geography, scoring three out of ten for history and four out of ten for geography. My overall position in class was fifth out of fifteen pupils.

In her report, Mrs Whitehead wrote: 'Angela works very well, but rather slowly. She maintains her position in class.' As a pupil I was, if nothing else, consistent, for all my school reports during primary school seemed to follow a similar pattern.

Morning break times meant only one thing: milk. And horrid it was, too: tepid, thin, sickly-sweet stuff, suffused with the chemical tang of cleaning disinfectant, handed out by the milk monitors, older pupils charged with the task of distributing bottles of this vile liquid. Drinking our enforced daily dose of milk was a trial to be endured; it left a stomach-churning, claggy aftertaste that is still memorable after all these years. Back then, the milk bottles were left unrefrigerated for hours, until it was time for the monitors to dish them out during mid-morning break. By the time the milk reached our lips, it was cloyingly warm – and, no doubt, bursting with bacteria.

Because the school was perched on a hill, the playground sloped downwards, which meant there was always a fair bit of huffing and puffing when we played our games of tig. I can recall playing a particular game of tig where we linked arms with someone and ran around the playground in search of someone else to tig so that our couple became a threesome, and then a foursome, and eventually expanded until there was a line of us. There would be other lines of children, all competing with each other to see who could get the biggest line. The game ended when every child was tigged. Running up and down that hill must have been very beneficial to our developing hearts and lungs, for I don't remember taking much time off school due to sickness, and I don't recall there being any overweight children in my class.

My favourite game was 'the farmer's in his den'. We would each link hands to form a circle, with one child – the farmer – in the middle. The farmer would then choose someone to be his wife, someone else to be his child, his dog and so on, until the circle grew ever smaller. It was a lovely, gentle game, and I can still remember the words we used to sing: 'The farmer's in his den, the farmer's in his den, ee-i-ad-i-o the farmer's in his den. The farmer wants a wife, the farmer wants a wife, ee-i-ad-i-o the farmer wants a wife...'

We used to walk the half mile or so to school every day, usually stopping at Granny's on the way home or calling at the Round House sweet shop. This was a sugar-lover's paradise, with row upon row of jars filled with every kind of sweet imaginable – wine gums, jelly babies, midget gems, liquorice sticks, chocolate buttons, sherbet dips, bubblegum gobstoppers ... all a source of childhood delight. As one of our treats we were allowed to buy a sixpenny bag of sweets. You could select your own goodies, and the kindly and patient shop assistant – who I think we called Mrs MacIntosh, though that may not have been her real name – would scoop them into a paper bag for us. More often than not, we'd choose love hearts, with their tangy, tingly taste, or space invaders, with their soft, sherbety insides.

During the school holidays, my brother and I would sometimes go to play at the joinery workshop that belonged to my dad and grandad. They started the business in Carr Lane, Pilling, in 1953, specialising in domestic joinery and carpentry before later branching out into commercial work.

The workshop was our very own adventure theme park, home to a fascinating array of industrial machines for splicing, sawing and smoothing wood, ready for crafting into windows, doors, roof trusses, shelves, skirting boards, cabinets and cupboards. There was always a pervasive smell of new wood, mingled with dust, and the floor was carpeted with sawdust and wood shavings which cushioned noise and gave the building its strange muffled acoustics.

At the flick of a switch, one of the mighty machines would roar in to life, letting off an ear-splitting, screeching sound that reverberated through the building. At the back of the workshop, a redundant hen cabin was an Aladdin's cave, filled to the brim with screws, nails, bolts, hinges, drills and all the paraphernalia of joinery. As children, we used to delight in playing shop. Dad would lay a length of plywood across a stack of bricks and this became our shop counter where we traded screws and nails. It kept us amused for hours.

Christmas at 19 Elletson Terrace was always an exciting time. It was a family affair shared with Granny and Grandad and Auntie Lizzie (Granny's sister) and her husband, Uncle Jack. The best part of Christmas was going to Thornton, a small town about six miles away, to pick up Auntie Lizzie and Uncle Jack and bring them over to our house so they could join in the festivities. My dad drove us in his slate-grey Austin A40. I don't know whether it was our mounting excitement, or the fact that the car was incapable of going much faster than 40 mph, but the journey to Auntie Lizzie's seemed to take forever. Auntie Lizzie and Uncle Jack worked at The Posy Bowl, a cafe owned by Dad's cousin, Adrienne, who lived in Thornton with her parents, Uncle Fred and Auntie Gladys. Uncle Fred was brother to Granny and Auntie Lizzie When it was time to go and collect Auntie Lizzie and Uncle Jack, there was mounting excitement because it meant one thing: Christmas was nearly upon us.

Crossing the River Wyre to get to Auntie Lizzie and Uncle Jack's meant going over the old Shard toll bridge, at Hambleton. This was a narrow toll bridge, linking the rural villages of Wyre to the rest of the world. Located at one end of the bridge was a toll booth, where there was nearly always a queue of cars waiting for tickets, slowing traffic down to a snail's pace. I can still see the tall, bespectacled elderly man in his bright yellow sou'wester coming out of the toll booth in the driving rain and wind, his ticket machine ready to take the money.

Drivers were charged according to the number of passengers in the car, children included, so it's perhaps not surprising that many canny mums and dads ordered their youngsters to crouch down behind the seats in the back of the vehicle, to dodge paying the toll.

Christmas morning followed a ritual that was as comfortable and familiar as an old overcoat. As children have since time immemorial, my brother and I would rise at dawn to find two bulging red stockings tied to the bedpost – a sure sign that Father Christmas had managed to find his way down our soot-clogged chimney, though he may well have burnt his toes landing on the dying embers of the coal fire that had cheerily burnt away in the grate hours earlier. We would spill out the contents of the stocking all over the eiderdown and happily amuse ourselves until our parents woke up. Each Christmas stocking came stuffed with an apple and a tangerine; a small bag of sweets; a small toy, perhaps a pencil case, or a Ladybird book; a bar of chocolate, perhaps a Toblerone or a Picnic bar; and a coin, usually a shilling. But we weren't allowed to open our Santa sacks – in reality, a pillowcase stuffed with toys – until after breakfast.

The great present-unwrapping ritual took place in the best living room, our front lounge reserved for special occasions. Mum and Dad watched and chortled with delight as we clamoured to tear open our presents, wrapped up in tissue-thin, gaudy paper. Presents were unsophisticated by today's standards – a game of snakes and ladders perhaps; or a drawing book; or a Plasticine set; or one of those delightful glass snow houses, where you shook it to produce a cascade of snowflakes. But they were always a source of delight, and they kept us amused for hours. I can remember asking Father Christmas for a doll. My wish was granted when I opened a parcel and found the biggest doll imaginable, with a mop of platinum-blonde curls. I christened her Valerie, and she immediately became my best friend.

Just before midday, it would be time to make the short walk to Granny's for her aforementioned Christmas feast, served up at twelve o'clock prompt. Grandad cautioned us not to get there too early because that would put Granny and her cook-in-arms, Auntie Lizzie, in to a fluster as they frantically scrambled around the bubbling saucepans and fussed over the turkey basting compliantly in the overworked stove.

After lunch had sent our digestive systems and our bodies sinking in to a sluggish, but satisfied, torpor, we would doze by the fire, waking up fully revived by four o'clock, full of the excitement and anticipation of visiting my mother's side of the family for a buffet tea. For this meant one thing: there would be more presents to unwrap. Christmas tea parties, usually hosted by Grandma, my mum's mother, or one of my aunties, were lively affairs, thronged with cousins and aunties and uncles and much raucous laughter. After tea, we'd all congregate around the TV to watch *The Black and White Minstrel Show* or *The Billy Cotton Band Show*, followed in later years by *Morecambe and Wise*, whose legendary shows in the late sixties and seventies became the staple of family Christmas viewing.

Knott End had its fair share of local characters; individuals renowned for their eccentricities who were part of the fabric of the community. One of these was Matt Danson, who delivered newspapers and was a familiar figure cycling round the village in his worsted coat and flat cap. 'Ay, ay,' he would call out cheerfully, doffing his cap as he made his way on his rounds. Matt was arguably the oldest paper*boy* in the area, delivering his newspapers until a ripe old age. He always referred to me as a little smiler. 'Ay, tha's a little smiler, thou art,' he'd say to my mum, grinning toothily as he stopped to talk to us on our way to school. As a child, I had plenty to smile about; life was generally carefree and idyllic.

4

'Come On Over to My Place'

'Where do you live?' people ask me. I usually hesitate a second or two before responding. If I say Preesall I'm invariably met with a puzzled frown and the inevitable question: 'Preesall? Where's that?' So it's easier to say Knott End. At this, some may show a glimmer of recognition. 'Ah, Knott End. Yes, I've heard of it, but isn't that the place where it reaches a dead end?'

What they are referring to is the inescapable fact that there's only one road in and out of Knott End. Travel to the farthest end of this road and you reach a natural end, the point of no return – the sea. This has given rise to Knott End's unfortunate sobriquet as 'dead end', the end of the world, the butt of many a comedian's wisecracks. But, in truth, this place has a colourful history that would defy the comics. Close your eyes, go back to the turn of the century, and imagine a thriving holiday and visitor resort … Take your mind back to the fifties and sixties, and imagine how Knott End danced to the rock 'n' roll beat … These aren't figments of the imagination, for lurking beneath its sedate exterior is the story of a village that's had a vibrant past, having undergone many identity changes.

If I close my own eyes, I can still picture the Knott End and Preesall of my childhood. It was an indisputably gentle place to live, and a safe, cosy backcloth for a nurtured and protected childhood. Back in the early sixties, Preesall was a small village with a separate identity from its neighbour, Knott End. The combined population of the two villages was around three thousand seven hundred. Today it's nearly double that, with close on six thousand residents.

Preesall boasted a plethora of small shops. There was a grocery store in Sandy Lane which used to sell everything from sweets and bread to coal and firewood. It was presided over by kindly Mrs Daniels. I can remember the thrill of being allowed to cross the main road from our house to buy sweets from her. I wouldn't have been much older than five at the time.

Next door to it was a shoe shop, tucked away in a small cabin behind the home of Ivor Miller, who used to sit on the wall outside his house in his trademark beige overcoat, waiting for custom. If you went there looking for fashion shoes you'd be disappointed; Ivor's range of footwear tended to be basic, restricted mainly to work shoes and wellington boots. As well as selling shoes he also repaired them. Inside his shop the distinctive smell of new leather mingled with the burning rubbery smell of shoes being lovingly restored. As with many families on a limited budget back then, it was much cheaper and easier for my mum to take our shoes to Ivor's to be repaired than to have to go out and buy a pair of new ones. I can also remember getting my first pair of wellies from him – in shiny, black rubber.

With my memories of Knott End back in the sixties a tad hazy, it was amazing what an hour's chat over a coffee with local historian Don Stringfellow could do. Talking to him brought back many images of shops and places that I'd forgotten even existed …

How can I forget Brown's Pharmacy, presided over by the eponymous Joe Brown (no relation to, and a world away from, his sixties singing counterpart), clinically garbed in a white coat and sporting a toothsome smile? His old-fashioned oak-panelled shop features a curious mix of lotions and potions, in an assortment of glass jars, designed to cure all ills, and there is always a smell of camphor. I'm here with my mother to buy Delrosa rosehip syrup. It's a thick, dark-red syrupy mixture, lauded by generations of families as a rich source of vitamin C. My mum promises it will keep us healthy and free of colds. Not that we really need much persuading, for it tastes delectably sweet.

There's the shoe shop in Wyre View, owned by Norman and Joyce Fisher, where my mum takes me to be fitted with Clarks shoes (we don't have much money, but when we are ready for new shoes she insists on us having the best in footwear). There's a fruit and vegetable shop, Berry's; an ironmongery run by the Mayman family; and there are two butchers. One of them, Gudgeon's, is presided over by florid-faced George Rawcliffe, famed for his pigeons and his ready repartee.

There's a ladies' fashion shop, specialising in ladies' and children's wear and an assortment of wools and knitting patterns, on Lancaster Road. It also sells women's foundation garments – corsets and girdles – by Playtex and Wolsey, as well as dress materials, bedding and curtain fabrics. Ah yes, it's all coming back to me now.

For women, foundation wear was seen as vital to creating a shapely figure. My mum was one of a generation of women who wouldn't leave the house without her tummy-flattening body armour: corsets in bone-encased strong satin, fastened with rows of hooks and eyes, and with those all-important garter straps for hoisting nylon stockings obediently in to place (women had yet to be liberated by that greatest ever invention – tights).

Perhaps not surprisingly, getting dressed was a major operation each morning. Thankfully, during my own growing up in the seventies we were free of such shackles, just as we were of many of the societal conventions imposed on our mothers' generation. It wasn't just tights that liberated us, but also a general loosening of attitudes towards women's roles that defined my generation, although we were still a long way removed from the girl-power generation of the present day.

My mum used to take me to Gladys Gee's hairdresser's to have my hair cut. Gladys was a bottle redhead and her husband a dapper little man in grey nylon overalls who helped in the shop, deftly brushing up the shorn hair carpeting the floor. They employed another hairdresser, Nancy, who was known for her waspish humour.

I used to chuckle inwardly at the rain hoods they gave to ladies to protect their hair from getting wet or windblown. They came in see-through plastic and fastened at the chin. It amused me to see women sauntering out of the hairdresser's after their customary wash and set, wearing what looked like a plastic bag over their immaculately coiffed hair. A wash and set meant having your hair washed and then 'set' in rollers. After a spell of being basted under the dome-shaped industrial dryer, your newly acquired curls were teased, backcombed and lacquered in to place. Sadly, the plastic rain hood did little to enhance your glamorous new hairdo, for it made you look like you were ready for being popped in to the freezer instead, hair frozen for posterity (yes, I know: I've stretched my writerly imagination a bit here, for the first freezers were still a decade or more away).

The undisputed epicentre of Knott End was the Verona Cinema, housed in what is now the Squash. The cinema was run by the redoubtable Mr and Mrs Miller, and became a magnet to cinemagoers from all over the district. It was very much a key part of my own teenage years, and so there will be much more about the Verona to follow in a later chapter.

Next to the Verona, in what is now the Spar store, was Lister's Cafe, selling groceries and confectionery, later becoming Green's. At some point during my childhood a local man, Jimmy Moss, took over the shop, running it with his family as a grocer and greengrocery shop.

Jimmy was also well known for his work as a chimney sweep, and he used to sweep our chimney in Elletson Terrace. During one visit, I can remember him telling my mum he could hear a strange noise. He thought there might be a cat stuck up the chimney. The fact that he repeated this on subsequent visits to sweep the chimney made her realise that he was having her on. Seemingly, my mum wasn't the only housewife to fall for this jape.

Behind Lister's was a barber's shop, run by Alan Smith. I can remember going there with my dad and brother, and being overpowered by the smell of Brylcreem.

'Do you remember the amusement arcade near the ferry slip?' asked Don, the local historian. Ah, now we're getting to the nitty-gritty of Knott End's claim to fame as the district's rock 'n' roll capital …

Situated on the Esplanade, at the end of Bourne May Road, just a few yards from the ferry terminal, the amusement arcade and jukebox were a major attraction for the hordes of visitors who spilt over in to Knott End from the Fleetwood–Knott End ferry.

The jukebox was launched during the early fifties after Joe Marshall built an ice-cream parlour on the car park of the motor vehicle repair garage, opposite the Bourne Arms pub. His pal Frank Wadsworth ran a novelty shop in a nearby block of shops. With the whole of Britain dancing to a new tune of post-war exuberance and optimism, the two friends decided to build the area's first jukebox. Within no time, it became a magnet for local teenagers.

In 1953, Jack Stringfellow – Don's father – bought the nearby coach business, Birch's Coaches, affectionately known as Birch's Bangers. At the same time, Jack's wife Doris took over the running of the jukebox.

As a child, I can vaguely remember the jukebox, the miniature rides and slot machines. But Raymond Fenton, one of those rock 'n' roll aficionados who used to swarm to the village, has vivid memories of the days Knott End rocked to the jukebox by the sea.

'We all used to congregate there on Saturdays,' he recalled. 'It was always packed out. For the price of a shilling you could have three plays on the jukebox. If you only wanted one play, it was sixpence.

'In the early days, it was The Everly Brothers, Elvis … all the fifties singers. We used to jive on the forecourt; they'd move all the slot machines back so that you had room to dance. Then we'd go to the cafe next door and have a coffee, because we weren't old enough to go in the pub.'

Raymond continued, 'There was a car park in front, so it was quite easy for all the bikers and the young lads with their old cars to find somewhere to park. The lads used to drive round in pre-war cars – Hillmans and such like. They were only worth about twenty quid; they only did about thirty miles per hour, chuffing and smoking and breaking down all the time. But at least they enabled people to get around to the dances that were popular at the time.

'And then came the sixties and along came the Beatles and I can still remember the jukebox playing "She Loves You" over and over again. And we'd all be singing and dancing and having the time of our lives. Knott End was definitely the place to be; it was really vibrant.'

The jukebox on the promenade wasn't the only rock 'n' roll venue in Knott End; the Verona Cinema also ran rock 'n' roll nights in its fifties heyday.

Further along the Esplanade was Kathleen Barton's shop, selling novelty goods, sweets, ice cream, tobacco, beach balls, buckets and spades, and sun hats, with a ladies' hairdresser's to the rear. I went there with my mum to buy a bucket and spade to play with on the beach. Back then, building sandcastles on the beach was a popular pastime for local families and visitors alike, though the sand was hardly of the soft, silky variety you might find in Blackpool and other resorts; it was sludgy and oily. We didn't give a thought to what horrors might be lurking on the sands: sewage, rubbish, or dead animals washed up on the incoming tide. Digging the compacted sand and piling it into buckets seemed a safe, clean, healthy pursuit. I certainly don't remember us suffering from any ill effects.

There was the popular café at the ferry, housed in the former Knott End-Garstang railway station. This was run by the Taylor family. Ramsay Taylor took over the business from his mother, Mrs C. T. Taylor, combining his work there with a vital community role as a leading member of Knott End's auxiliary coastguard. Today the café is still going strong, though now housed in a swish modern building, with Ramsay's son and daughter-in-law, Steve and Jean, at the helm.

Other cafes of the day included Lister's, in the centre of Knott End, with its motto: 'You'll like the fare, and you'll fare as you like at Lister's!' There was Ormerod's fish and chip restaurant in Wyre View. Visitors to Preesall could pop in to Prospect Cafe, in Smithy Lane, operated by Mrs M. Pammenter, for luncheon, tea or home-made cakes.

And if that wasn't enough, there was the fleet of grocery vans that motored up and down the leafy lanes of our Over Wyre district, providing a door-to-door service, keeping locals supplied with fish, meat, bread and assorted other goods. The drivers were always good-natured souls who knew all their customers. Don Stringfellow can recall the days when Knott End and Preesall were served by no fewer than eleven travelling shops. Among these were Hogg's, from the nearby village of Great Eccleston, who specialised in selling boots, shoes and wellingtons!

One mobile shopkeeper who sticks out in my memory is Jim Cross. I can remember him calling at our house in his green van, stocked with everything from fresh bread and bananas to medicine and even firewood and paraffin oil. Cheery Jim was a familiar figure as he made his daily rounds touring farms and cottages in the villages of Knott End, Preesall, Pilling and the tiny hamlet of Eagland Hill.

His working day stretched out much longer than it should have done because his customers kept offering him cups of tea! My mum was one such housewife who loved to chat to him, and he always found time to talk to my brother and me, asking us what we'd been up to at school. Jim worked long after retirement age, until competition from the big supermarkets, in the late sixties, forced him to hang up his overcoat.

It's interesting to see how the advent of online shopping has led to the revival of the mobile shop, seen in the proliferation of Tesco vans and the like. But it makes you wonder how many of our modern-day delivery drivers would have the time for a cup of tea and a chat – and be on first-name terms with all their customers, as Jim was.

5

'The Times they are A-Changing'

The walk to school should have taken about twenty minutes, but for a dawdler like me this could easily stretch to half an hour or more. Aged six, I was entrusted by my parents to walk to school with my friends, and we would saunter up the hill as if we had all the time in the world, stopping off to stroke a pony peering over the fence or play chase through the fields. Back then there were fields on either side of the road leading up to Fordstone Bridge, the old railway bridge. To the right you could see the track line made by the disused Knott End–Garstang railway, cutting a swathe through the grass and hedgerows, across the landscape that has remained unchanged to this day. To the left was a cornfield that stretched out for what, to our tiny eyes, seemed like miles.

But one day, sometime during the early sixties, something happened that changed our little corner of the world forever. It wasn't exactly *The Day of the Triffids*; more like The Day of the Bulldozers: the day the bulldozers and an army of builders invaded. Within what seemed like no time at all, the cornfield was churned up – and a crop of bungalows and houses sprouted from beneath the fertile acres. Shops followed, and then a patchwork of roads. And soon those green pastures metamorphosed in to a sprawling concrete paddock that became known as the Fordstone Avenue estate, unfurling before our eyes.

Fordstone wasn't the first estate. Towards the end of the

fifties new bungalows surfaced on pastures near Knott End's golf course, their impact barely felt at first. But eventually swathes of land lying beside the sea were gobbled up by developers and cultivated into sprawling masses of identikit bungalows. Among these was the grand-sounding Links estate, so called because of its proximity to the links golf course. Elsewhere, dozens of purpose-built retirement bungalows were planted, like arable crops, on lands nudging the coast. Out of these sprung The Lakes estate, its fancy road names – Coniston Avenue, Grasmere Road, Rydal Road – conjuring an image of bucolic bliss. But nothing could disguise its impact on our once green and pleasant lands.

I can remember watching the fields of my childhood being swallowed up with an almost morbid fascination. Many folk muttered and moaned about the size of these housing developments, my own family included; they were dubbed, unkindly, by some locals as 'Kelly's Islands' after Samuel Kelly, the Manchester-based builder who created them. Perhaps, understandably, people were worried about what would happen when an invasion of 'offcomers' moved in.

'They'll just want to take over,' said my granny, echoing the concerns of many who feared a mass community takeover by an army of 'townies.'

It was no secret that the housing estates were designed with one purpose in mind: to lure people from towns such as Bolton, Manchester, Bury and Oldham to a retirement haven beside the sea, with the seductive promise of a few golden years basking in Knott End's health-giving properties before life's final sunset. Which meant my granny might well have had a point.

However, lest anyone should accuse our family, or others in our community, of being prejudiced against town dwellers, it's probably fair to say that the influx of newcomers back then, and since, has injected new life into a community that might otherwise have become insular and stultifying. Over time, we sand grown 'uns – those of us who were born in the district – grew to accept the new folk. After all, it wasn't as if they had two heads, or were bringing some kind of dreaded disease into our precious lands! Most arrivals, we soon discovered, held the same ideals that we did – wanting nothing more than a quiet life beside the sea, away from the hurly-burly of urban life. As time wore on, many local families also moved in to the new bungalows.

For anyone who might have had doubts about moving in to the area, the official guide to Knott End and Preesall gave plenty of reasons to convince people why it was such an attractive place to live, extolling the health benefits of Knott End's bracing sea breezes:

Fleetwood ... has always been prominent in sunshine records, and has twice led the field among northern resorts; since Knott End and Fleetwood rub shoulders, so to speak ... it follows that Knott End (and Preesall, of course) share this factor. The cold east winds are warded off by the Pennines and the climate is ... equable, braced by invigorating sea breezes; the very healthy and bracing atmosphere of the district has, in fact, often led to its adoption as a place of residence on medical recommendations.

Living the retirement dream was easy on the pocket, as well. Back in the early sixties, a two-bedroom semi-detached bungalow with garage space started at a cool £1,695. So popular was the district that prices rose, with later advertisements featuring a two-bedroomed semi-detached bungalow for £3,395 rising to £3,600 for a three-bedroom semi-detached dormer with garage space.

Even Coronation Street played its part in promoting Knott End as a retirement resort! During the first episode in 1960, Elsie Lappin announced she would be moving to a retirement home in Knott End after selling the corner shop to Florrie Lindley.

The fields of my sixties childhood may have long-since disappeared, but Knott End hasn't been a stranger to change over the past century or more, having undergone several incarnations. A peek into Don Stringfellow's historical records reveals how, back in the twenties, Knott End was a thriving holiday resort, boasting more than twenty boarding houses, each doing a roaring trade for visitors wanting to escape bigger and brasher resorts like Blackpool, Fleetwood and Cleveleys, in search of somewhere more genteel.

Alongside these, many other privately owned houses on Knott End's sea front were rented out for holiday use. Preesall resident Marion Williamson can remember her mother opening up the family home, in Parrox View, to visitors. Guests would bring their own food to save costs, and Marion's mother would cook their meals for them. She charged 42s for a week's stay, which included breakfast and tea. During wakes weeks, there was always a flurry of visitors from the industrial towns such as Blackburn, Burnley and Bolton.

Visitors swarmed into the district on the Fleetwood–Knott End ferry boat which operated continuously, carrying up to forty thousand passengers per week (see more about the ferry in the next chapter). Or they would hop on the Pilling Pig – the famed little train, so called because of its whistle which sounded like a squealing pig – which chugged along the eleven-mile Knott End–Garstang railway track.

The official guide, produced by Preesall Urban District Council, did a grand job of selling Knott End's attractions, listing reasons why people should visit the district, not least because of the unspoilt nature of the district and countryside, the bracing climate and the close proximity to Blackpool.

Sadly, it was the introduction of motor cars that led to Knott End's demise as a holiday resort. Passenger numbers on the ferry and railway began to drop as people discovered the convenience of owning their own car. With their new-found independence they began to venture further afield, discovering new destinations. Owning a car opened up the wider vistas offered by Lake District, Scotland, and the Yorkshire Dales.

Gradually, over a number of years, the boarding houses on the prom dwindled and they were eventually converted in to private houses. Knott End settled down to its new identity, becoming a quiet residential area. But all that changed in the sixties, with the explosion of housebuilding that led to the district reinventing itself as a retirement resort.

Over the years the scale of development has continued, and today the district is unrecognisable from the place I grew up in as a child. Gone are the fields that separated Knott End from its near-neighbour, Preesall; now it's hard to know exactly where Preesall ends and Knott End begins, for the two have virtually merged in to one small coastal community. Arguably, though, it remains a quiet, peaceful and pleasant place to live, although there are many who feel that the scale of development has gone far enough.

As I write this, the district of my birth is poised for unprecedented change that will alter the landscape and character of the community. A major project to store gas in underground caverns on the banks of the River Wyre has been approved. There are proposals to build a new tidal barrage across the Wyre Estuary to Fleetwood. On top of this, many services, including local bus services, the youth centre and the historic Knott End–Fleetwood ferry are faced with the axe, because of council cutbacks. There's no doubt each of these changes will have a major impact on residents. But as history has shown, Knott End and Preesall have undergone many changes of identity over the past century or more. Like the shifting sands, and the ebbing and flowing of the tide, the fortunes of my community have fluctuated over the years – very much like life itself.

6

Ferry 'Cross the Wyre

Gerry and the Pacemakers sang fondly of their 'Ferry 'Cross the Mersey' but back in the sixties it was our own ferry 'cross the Wyre that chugged along happily in the waters of the Wyre, transporting passengers to and fro between Knott End and its brash big sister, Fleetwood. The ferry predates the sixties, of course, with its long history stretching back to the late 1800s. But it played a big part in my sixties childhood – and its anchors are rooted even deeper in my family's past.

I can remember the excitement of climbing aboard the little ferry boat for a day out to Fleetwood with Granny; it was always a huge treat for my brother and me. Stepping aboard was a real balancing act and could be fraught with danger; you had to clamber over a makeshift platform with extreme caution, or risk falling in the water lying in the gap between the bobbing boat and the Knott End jetty, the long stretch of land edging down to the water's edge – more often referred to locally as the 'ferry slip.'

Once aboard the boat, you were at the mercy of the weather. Most of the seating was outside on the open deck, where you were exposed to the elements – the wind, and waves crashing and hurtling across from the Irish Sea. There was a small covered area below deck, close to the engine room, but seats were restricted.

The short crossing was always great fun; sometimes it would be wild and windy, and you would be tossed and pitched as the boat danced wildly with the waves. At other times you hardly knew you were moving as the vessel glided over the calm, low-lying tidal waters flanked by the wide expanse of caramel sands.

When we reached Fleetwood we would go to the tiny beach near the ferry terminal, armed with bucket and spade. Or we might walk to the Marine Hall Gardens for an ice cream, and later Granny would let us loose on the playground. I can remember the time my brother caused consternation when he decided to walk down the helter-skelter, rather than slide on his bottom. I still have images of him perched precariously at the top of the helter-skelter, mat in hand, beginning his descent, much to Granny's horror.

'Sit down or you'll fall!' Granny pleaded as she peered up anxiously. Soon she was joined by an equally anxious fairground operator who began to clamber up the railings with monkey-like agility. Thankfully, at that point, my brother saw the wisdom of sliding down on his bottom, receiving a good telling-off as he landed.

Long before I was born, the ferry played a role in my family. During the thirties and forties, Uncle Jack Wright – husband of Granny's sister, Auntie Lizzie – worked for the Fleetwood–Knott End ferry operators as the sweeper of the tide. This might not have been his official job title, but it was his role to sweep away water and debris from the ferry slip, allowing passengers to disembark from the ferry boat in comfort and safety.

It's true what they say: time and tide wait for no man, not even for my Uncle Jack. Sweeping away the silted tidal water with little more than a long-handled sweeping brush was back-breaking and often futile work. The ferry operators, recognising the difficulty of the task, eventually bought him a motor-operated pump with an adjustable hose. It was meant to work in a similar way to a lawnmower, but it turned out to be more trouble than it was worth; an onlooker who used to watch Uncle Jack struggling to get the motor started recalled how it took him so long to get the thing going it would have been easier for him to have carried on using his brush!

Uncle Jack, in his long, white sea boots, nautical navy blue jumper and matching trousers, was a well-known figure on the ferry slip. During foggy weather he carried a large handbell which he would ring as loudly as possible in order to guide the boat safely across the dense water. With thousands of visitors piling off the ferry boat every week during the summer months, it was also part of his job to assist holidaymakers in unloading their luggage, helping to lug suitcases on to a waiting handcart, ready to dispatch the holiday items to nearby hotels and boarding houses.

His wife, my Auntie Lizzie, worked in the ticket office, located in a wooden hut near the top of the ferry slip. In the waiting room a pot-bellied stove blazed merrily, a welcome sight for passengers on cold winter mornings. Naturally, this was all before my time, but I like to think my family have played a tiny part in the ferry's colourful history.

Of course, lots of people have their own stories to tell of the Fleetwood–Knott End ferry service, no one more so than Bob Croft, whose ancestors provided the forerunner to the service, back in the mid 1800s. Brothers John, Robert and Thomas Croft ran their own rowing boat pleasure trips across the river in the days before the ferry. Later Fleetwood Council, eyeing up the potential for profit, launched a commercial ferry business. Eventually, the Croft family were employed to operate the vessel.

In its early days the ferry linked the agricultural community of Over Wyre with Fleetwood Market, transporting livestock as well as people. Picture the scene: it's a busy market day and crowds throng the beach. Farmers wait to board the boat, carrying their cargo of bewildered hens in wooden crates. Young men push handcarts laden with vegetables and fruit. Frisky cattle and ponies jostle for position, led along by their owners. As the boat arrives, passengers and livestock pile on. All, that is, except for the cattle and horses who are herded in to the river, halters attached, and forced to swim behind the boat across the watery pastures of the Wyre.

Pilling farmer Norman Bleasdale, who lived until the grand age of ninety-seven, could recall visiting Fleetwood Market each Friday when he was a young man, just after the First World War. He used to pull a cart brimming with apples, pears and plums from the farm, ready to be sold on the market.

Norman remembered the fateful night the ferry boat got lost while carrying its young passengers from Fleetwood Grammar School back to their homes in Over Wyre. On this particular winter's evening the vessel became enveloped in a thick blanket of fog as it set sail from Fleetwood. The skipper became disorientated and lost his sighting of the Knott End slipway. Meanwhile, parents of the grammar school pupils kept a night-time vigil on the slipway, clutching storm lamps and anxiously looking out over the Wyre Estuary for the lost boat. A full evening passed and there was no sign. By this time the parents were getting frantic.

Twelve hours later, as daylight dawned, the little boat reappeared through the rising fog, its passengers miraculously unscathed from their unscheduled night at sea, and watching parents said their prayers and thanked God for the miracle that had prevented the boat from hitting a sand bank or, worse, drifting out to the unforgiving waters of the Irish Sea.

Another Pilling farmer, John Higginson, can recall how his mother and aunts used to smuggle black market bacon across the ferry in potato hampers – wicker carts – during the Second World War. The illicit bacon, produced in contravention of rationing regulations, would be concealed in the hamper under layers of damsons or vegetables being taken to be sold at Fleetwood Market. The meat would be bartered to the stallholders in exchange for other black market goods, such as sugar or flour.

As a child growing up in the forties, Bob Croft can remember making regular trips across to Fleetwood on the ferry boat with his grandmother, Beatrice. So popular was the ferry back then that three vessels – the Wyresdale, Lunevale and reserve boat, the Calder Vale – were needed to transport the hundreds of passengers across the river every day.

'There'd be queues, four or five abreast, of people waiting on the ferry slip at Fleetwood to get across the water to Knott End,' he recalled. 'My grandma would hold my hand and she'd just march straight to the head of the queue, saying, "We're local," and Bob Wright, the skipper, would say, "All right, Beattie, on you get." I used to feel very embarrassed even at that tender age.'

The young Bob was thrilled when the captain invited him to go up to the bridge deck, to watch what was going on. 'I used to watch what he was doing and I took it all in, even though I was only a kid. I was absolutely fascinated by all the turns and manoeuvres and, even though I come from a family of seafarers, it was going on the ferry boats that made me decide on a career in sailing.'

My Auntie June, my mum's sister, was one of several generations of Over Wyre pupils who caught the ferry each day to go to Fleetwood Grammar School during the fifties. She can remember making the crossing in all weathers, including stormy days when the wind whipped up waves and the boat tossed and turned with heady abandon. During these exceptionally rough conditions, pupils were ordered to stay downstairs in the inside cabin.

Another with memories of making the daily ferry crossing to school is Pat Kershaw (formerly Clutton). She recalls: 'It was very rare for the boat not to run, even when the weather was rough. If it was really wet and windy we'd be wet through by the time we reached school, but we didn't mind that because it meant the teachers gave us tea and toast to warm up!'I don't remember ever getting a cold or taking time off school – I think it made us hardier.

'If the tide was really low, you'd have to jump off the boat and on to the ferry slip. And that could be a bit scary sometimes, because you were always frightened you might fall in the river.'

For Peter and Judith Atkinson, the little boat unwittingly played cupid to their romance back in the fifties. Judith recalls how, as a young teacher, she was visiting Fleetwood to collect some books. Heavy fog delayed the return boat crossing to Knott End. Peter Atkinson, on leave from the merchant navy, was also among the passengers that day. As they waited for the fog to clear, Judith and Peter got talking. One thing led to another, and eventually they married – and to this day remain thankful for the part the ferry played in their romance.

Fast forward to the present day: the future of the ferry service is in jeopardy, having become the victim of council cutbacks. It isn't the first time its demise has been threatened. Over the years, the fate and fortunes of the little vessel may have ebbed and flowed, but for many sand grown 'uns like myself the ferry is as much a part of the fabric of Knott End as the sea and the sands and the ceaseless tide. The thought of losing such a colourful slice of our heritage makes me feel desperately sad; it almost feels as if I'm losing a tiny part of myself, my family history and my identity, a sentiment that is certain to be echoed by many.

7

'Day Tripper'

As children, it was a real treat to go with Mum to Blackpool on the number 85 red double-decker Ribble bus, operating from Knott End to Blackpool's Talbot Road bus station. Preesall and Knott End might have been self-sufficient as far as shops and shopping were concerned, but that didn't stop us from venturing to town to visit the big department stores, such as Timothy Whites, British Home Stores and, of course, Marks and Spencer.

The bus would meander along country lanes, the journey punctuated by the bus conductor in a jaunty black cap, ticket machine strapped across the shoulder, making his way (for it was usually a man, back then) down the aisles, requesting each passenger have ready their 'penny for the bridge.' This was to cover the penny fare to cross the Shard Bridge, for even bus passengers weren't exempt from toll charges. Arriving at what, to us, was the great metropolis of Blackpool, we sometimes used to get off the bus early, just before the Devonshire Road traffic lights, so that my mum could stop off at George Blackburn's store. This was an independently run fabric shop, filled with every kind of fabric imaginable. My mum, being a keen dressmaker, loved to browse through all the different shades and patterns of material.

In the sixties, Blackpool blossomed as a holiday resort and as a shopping centre. It boasted many of its own iconic department stores such as gracious R.H.O. Hills, which later became Binns, and stylish Lewis's with its distinctive turquoise tiled facade. Opened in 1964, Lewis's stood as a proud beacon to all that was vibrant and exciting about sixties fashion and pop culture.

Even traditional department stores like British Home Stores had a very different feel than today: the floor space was dominated by glass-fronted display counters. On one counter there would be bundles of neatly folded jumpers and cardigans, wrapped in polythene covers. Other counters would specialise in underwear or toiletries, stacked in tidy rows. Standing sentry-like behind each counter, the shop assistants, in nylon overalls, unfailingly addressed customers as 'sir' or 'madam.' You would select the item you wanted and pay for it at the till at your chosen counter. Looking back, it was all very formal and old-fashioned – redolent of the Grace Brothers' department store in *Are You Being Served?* – lacking the soft lighting, the enticing displays and the inviting, touchy-feely ambience of the artfully designed stores of today.

Blackpool could also justifiably claim the title as the show-business capital of the north, hosting a galaxy of big-name stars: Cilla Black, The Bachelors, Freddie and the Dreamers, and Cliff Richard were among those to grace the resort. The Winter Gardens, the Opera House and the ABC were premier entertainment venues, bursting with showbiz glamour unrivalled anywhere outside London.

I can remember going to see Kathy Kirby and Frank Ifield at the Opera House with my mum, dad and brother. I would have been about six at the time. Kathy Kirby was a Marilyn Monroe lookalike, famed for songs such as 'Secret Love', 'Miss Lipgloss' and 'Body and Soul.' A few years later Mum took us to the ABC to see Tom Jones and, later, Englebert Humperdink top the bill at the height of their fame.

Growing up a half-hour bus ride away from Blackpool, there was always a sense of excitement about our visits, and a palpable sense of fun and glamour and glitz associated with the resort.

Back then it all seemed so much more wholesome: the donkey rides; the deckchairs stretched out across the sands; the trams zipping up and down the promenade; the celebrity shows; the exciting shops. Although it's easy to look on the past with the fuzzy warmth of nostalgia, there are many who would argue that Blackpool today, with its unfortunate image as the dubious capital of stag and hen weekends, is a pale and somewhat jaded version of its sixties self, with its shabby amusement arcades, greasy burger bars and tired bingo halls. However, a new pedestrianised walkway has revitalised part of the promenade.

Aside from our trips to Blackpool, we used to go on outings with Grandma and Grandad Bill, travelling in Grandad Bill's old blue Ford Popular. As a real treat, we would go for lunch to The Fernhill, a gracious country house, owned by the pint-sized comedian Jimmy Clitheroe, a household name then. Sunday lunch would be traditional fare: roast beef and Yorkshire pudding with all the trimmings, followed by apple pie and custard.

It was standard, plain no-frills food; we were still to savour the experience of continental dishes like pizza, lasagne, moussaka and, heaven forbid, garlic bread! Unlike today, with dining out a regular pastime, going somewhere for lunch was a rare and special treat, one that we relished, along with the fancy napkins, napery, silver service and sense of occasion that went along with it. After lunch, we'd go for a drive to the Trough of Bowland, Grandad Bill's Ford Popular chuttering along the narrow, twisting inclines at 25 mph.

Today it is sad to see that The Fernhill, once a beacon of refined elegance epitomising an era of glamour and sophistication, is no more, having been flattened by the bulldozer and replaced by three modern detached dwellings that still bear for-sale signs more than two years on.

The highlight of our year took place right on our doorstep. Knott End and Preesall Gala was held on the second Saturday in July. The gala took place on Parrox Hall field and was the focal point of community life, drawing grandparents, parents, children and babies from across the Over Wyre villages. A procession, led by Pilling Jubilee Silver Band, would assemble at the Bourne Arms in Knott End, before snaking its way along the three-mile route through Knott End and Preesall, to the delight of cheering onlookers.

Hundreds of people gathered to watch the crowning of the gala queen in the shadow of a magnificent oak tree on the Parrox field, flanked by stately Parrox Hall. My Auntie June, my mum's sister, has fond memories of being chosen for the regal honour in 1954. After the crowning of the queen, everyone would join in a packed programme of activities on the field, including three-legged and egg-and-spoon races, donkey rides and fairground rides.

My family was involved in the organisation of the gala: Granny and Grandad were members of Preesall Athletics Club, who ran the gala in the years after the war. It was tradition to invite someone well known to open the festivities – usually someone who was appearing in Blackpool for the summer season. I can remember one year, the children's madcap entertainer Mr Pastry (the late actor Richard Hearne) agreed to open the gala and my dad went to pick him up from Blackpool Opera House in his Morris Minor. It felt very thrilling and exciting to think of Mr Pastry, star of stage and screen, travelling in *our* car. He was the latest in a line-up of celebrities invited to perform the opening ceremony, sharing honours with illustrious names including Max Bygraves and George Formby.

Today, Knott End and Preesall Gala is still going strong though, as with many carnivals and festivals, its future depends on the commitment and time of an ever-dwindling band of volunteers, and the enthusiasm and willingness of local people to take part in the fun. Sadly, as seems to be the way with these things, the numbers have fallen by the wayside in recent years. In an era of time deprivation and increasing competition from more sophisticated forms of entertainment offered by theme parks, multiplex cinemas and the internet, it remains to be seen how long the gala can survive. I fervently hope it can keep going for future generations to enjoy.

In 1965, there was a dramatic change in my life. Mum and Dad announced that we would be leaving Elletson Terrace. The house had belonged to Auntie Lizzie and Uncle Jack, and they wanted to retire from their work at the Posy Bowl Cafe and return to their home. We were fortunate because, at the same time, a house belonging to my grandad's relatives became available. It needed renovation but it was perfect for a family. It meant we would have to move to a new house and a new life – in Pilling! A new chapter in my life was about to begin.

8

'The Times they are A-Changing' Again

Vine Cottage in School Lane, Pilling, was built in 1844. We moved there in January 1965, and it was to be my home for the next chunk of my childhood and teenage years. But long before we decamped there my gurgling tummy told its own tale of anxiety. To my eight-year-old eyes, it was like a ghost house: full of dark corners, cold, damp, and creepy. As a young visitor I would never venture away from the living room, fearful of what nasties might confront me in its cobwebby nooks and crannies.

The house had belonged to my grandad's aunts – Auntie Mary and Auntie Alice – who lived there up until their deaths in the early sixties. They were sisters of my dad's grandfather, Henry Alty. His widow, Elizabeth Alty, lived in the wooden bungalow adjoining the house with her daughter, Freda, my dad's auntie.

Before moving to Vine Cottage we used to visit the aunts on a regular basis. I was terrified of them. Looking back, they were in all probability kindly, benevolent, gentle old ladies. But to my wary young eyes they resembled witches with their stooped posture, straggly hair and missing teeth. The dark, brooding atmosphere in the house added to my sense of unease; the living room was a dimly lit cavernous room with a flagstone floor, and one side was dominated by a huge blackened fire range where there was always a roaring fire, even in summer. At the back of the house was a cobbled courtyard, flanked by stables. In the middle of the yard lay a disused well, several feet deep and deemed too dangerous for inquisitive children. There was no running water, gas or electricity. It was like something out of a Charles Dickens novel.

When the aunts died, my parents were offered the chance to move there. They set about transforming it into a family home, working during the evenings and weekends to convert the dark, musty cobweb-lined rooms into a home that was modern and habitable and yet retained the character of a nineteenth-century cottage. Out went the old-fashioned fire range; in came an Italian marble tiled fireplace with a slate hearth, in keeping with the sixties era of bold new designs. The old flagstones were taken up and replaced by a new asphalt floor, which was then carpeted.

Years before we moved in, two rooms at the front of Vine Cottage had been rented out to a local GP, Dr Andrew Taylor, for use as a village surgery; there was a waiting room on one side and a consulting room on the other. When our family took over, my dad converted what used to be the front room doctor's waiting area into an elegant hallway complete with a new parquet floor – my mother's pride and joy. The kitchen was gutted and Grandad Bob fitted new cupboards and a long fold-up breakfast bar that was probably ahead of its time. At the front, gleaming new French windows were installed at my mum's behest, but the old sash windows, with their tiny square panels, were retained to ensure the house kept its quaint cottagey feel.

The old well that stood outside at the back was filled in, and we said farewell to the cobblestone courtyard. Though this had added to the character of Vine Cottage, it was deemed impractical for our modern sixties family. The cobblestones were removed and the area grassed over to create a spacious back garden. The old stables were transformed in to a play den where my brother and I, and our friends, would spend many happy hours playing shop and organising 'concerts.' A wooden plank stretched across two chairs became a makeshift stage, complete with stage curtains made from an old cotton sheet draped from the ceiling. An old upright piano completed the scene, and we devised our own theatrical productions, performed to an audience made up of our parents and Granny and Grandad.

Being uprooted from our home in Preesall and moving to a new village was a massive upheaval. The three miles that separated Pilling from Preesall could have been half the world away as far as we were concerned, for it meant leaving behind all our friends at Preesall Fleetwood Charity School and starting afresh.

My new school, St John's CE Primary School, was just down the road from where we lived, a five-minute walk away. I was following in the footsteps of my grandad, Bob France, who had been a pupil there. On my first day I was ordered to go to Mrs Mitchell's class, which was the lower juniors' class. A platinum blonde, Mrs Mitchell was a kindly, softly spoken teacher who bred horses in her spare time and wore 'trews' that looked very much like jodhpurs.

My first day at school was memorable because there was another new starter, a very shy blond-haired boy from Manchester, dressed in fawn-coloured shorts. He was the son of the new village policeman, PC Ted Norris, who had transferred to Pilling from Swinton, Manchester, with his family of five children in order to give them a better life. I didn't realise this at the time, but over the years, the lives of Keith Norris and I would run parallel to each other. But on that first day there was nothing in the demeanour of this quiet boy to suggest that he would have any significance in my life.

Back then, each village had its own resident police officer, located in the police house. For Ted Norris, moving from inner-city crime-ridden Manchester to the quiet rural backwater of Pilling must have been a big culture shock, not least because there was very little crime, save for the occasional speeding offence. Despite this, he soon settled in to his new role and quickly gained a reputation as the village's friendly local bobby.

Pilling School was a quintessential old-fashioned village primary school with an interesting history. It was built in 1856 at a cost of £1,300, wrote former head teacher R.J. Sobee in his illustrious book, *A History of Pilling*, published in 1953. According to his records, children from non-farming families were ordered to pay £10 per year for the education of each child. For some inexplicable reason, children from farming families had to pay an additional charge of 1d per week to learn how to read, write and do arithmetic.

Sobee describes how, at that time, it wasn't unusual for some of the pupils to opt out of school during the summer and resume their education in the winter. During the summer months many of the youngsters were busily engaged in the art of 'wheat begging' – visiting one farmhouse after another to obtain a few handfuls of wheat. Apparently, this was considered by parents to be a much more profitable use of time than their offspring's education!

Alas, during my days at Pilling School we didn't have wheat begging to keep us away from school, and my parents would have baulked at the cost of paying towards my education. It's probably fair to say that my first year or two at Pilling School were as relaxed and carefree as a donkey ride on Blackpool sands. There was no national curriculum, nor did we have SATs, or any tests of any kind, save for the weekly spelling test. A generous dollop of time was devoted to outdoor activities such as rounders and skipping rope games in the yard.

Mrs Mitchell imbued in us a love of nature. She encouraged us to collect acorns, chestnuts, flowers, shells, leaves and seeds for the nature table, which took pride of place in the classroom. Thanks to an old-fashioned radio, we could listen to the music education programme, *Singing Together*, and sing with gusto to anthems such as 'Shanandoah' and 'When the Saints Go Marching In.' The wireless also acted as a substitute PE teacher during the *Music and Movement* programme, when a disembodied voice from the loudspeaker crackled out instructions on how many bunny-hops, skips, jumps or forward rolls we had to perform, all to accompanying backing music. Oh yes, it was an easy life for our teachers – and for us as well – devoid of league tables and Ofsted inspections. I remember my first couple of years at Pilling School as being really happy ones.

Adjoining the school was the head teacher's house. Separating the junior classroom (Mrs Mitchell's class) from the top class (Mr Shelley's) was a glass partition. In his book, Sobee records how one of the classrooms housed a gallery, where the naughty children were sent. But this was regarded as anything but a punishment by the young mischief-makers, who used to delight in pushing pencils through the gap in the gallery floor, making sure they landed torpedo-like on the heads of pupils sitting below. Apparently, pupils would compete to see how often they could be banished to the gallery!

The gallery was removed in 1893. During my days at primary school, there was no evidence of it ever having been there. But I wonder whether it was the ghostly echoes of those young scallions that was behind the throwing of paper aeroplanes and the fountain-pen bombing (when kids would splat each other with ink) of my own school-day contemporaries?

At the back of the school was a spacious playground, dominated by two former air-raid shelters; these served as makeshift goalposts for the lads during playtime football kick-abouts. Next to the playground were outside toilets. These got progressively bigger the older you were; the infant toilets were tiny and then as you progressed to juniors they were almost adult-sized. Making a trip to the loo wasn't a nice experience, especially in winter when it was cold and damp. The dampness seemed to permeate the walls, creating a musty smell mingled with the odour of disinfectant. Nor did the toilet paper with its rough texture, similar to tracing paper only harder and colder, and the foul-smelling carbolic soap, do anything to make the experience enticing.

My best friend at school was Anne Rossall, a rosy-faced, jolly girl who lived across the road from me, at Village Farm. Her parents, Bob and Hilda, also became friendly with my parents. As a child, I spent many idyllic days playing on the farm. We would go blackberry picking in the fields; watch the cows being milked; squeal with delight at the sight of newborn piglets suckling; gather eggs from the hen cabins; chase each other around the orchard; and race through the cowsheds. Even today, the soft sweet, muffled scent of hay mingled with the pungent, unmistakable aroma of cow dung takes me back to those times when we'd traipse through the barns to stroke the young calves gazing over at us with their big doleful eyes.

Bob and Hilda treated our family very kindly, opening their home and their hearts to us. At this point we no longer had a car, my dad having swapped his Austin A40 for a van, in order to run his joinery business. Generously, Bob and Hilda would give up their time to treat my mother, Geoff and me to days out. Bob, kind and gentle, would drive us to the Lakes in his Ford Zodiac, purring along the winding lanes. We'd go for a walk or a picnic, and then we'd set off back, making the journey home in time for milking the cows in the early evening. That was always the stipulation for our days out: we had to be back in time for milking.

At that time it was every little girl's dream to own a pony. I was no exception; I pestered and pleaded with my parents to let me have one, but it was to no avail.

'Where would you keep a pony?' was my mum's oft-repeated response. 'And who would look after it?' When Anne's parents bought her a placid grey mare, I felt pangs of envy. But I quickly grew to love that pony, named Silver, almost as much as her owner did. Anne was fearful of riding Silver, but I had no such qualms and would happily sit astride her and trot with her at a gentle pace around the farmyard, led by a nervous Hilda. Because I was small, in comparison to Silver, I had to stand on a wooden crate in order to mount the pony.

Sadly, after a few years, Silver developed a tumour behind her left eye and had to have her eye removed. I was with Anne and her parents when they took her to the Royal Veterinary Hospital in Liverpool to have her operation. Later, Silver returned to the farm with her eye missing but her gentle spirit intact and she managed to live out her years in equine harmony in the orchard adjoining the farm. Alas, though, I was never able to ride her again.

Though my parents resisted my pleas for a pony of my own, as a concession they allowed me to keep some bantams. These were Light Sussex bantams with distinctive white coats and black-and-white plumage. I managed to tame them and literally had them eating out of my hands, feeding them grain as they perched on the handle of the lawnmower. They made delightful pets and, of course, they kept us supplied with lovely eggs.

Unlike Knott End and Preesall, the character of Pilling hasn't changed radically since the sixties, save for a few small housing estates that have sprung up here and there, namely Broadfleet Close and Stakepool Drive, and infill detached houses and bungalows that have mushroomed up along Smallwood Hey Road, Lancaster Road and Garstang Road.

Today the village is still the same sleepy, sprawling village I can remember from my childhood. It has retained its village identity and clings to its centuries-old traditions and customs. Typical of these is the annual Coffee Feast Day, held each July, with roots going back to the days when coffee was considered a luxury commodity. During the early coffee feast days it was customary to drink coffee.

Like Knott End and Preesall, and I suspect many other villages up and down the country, Pilling had its share of 'characters': individuals known for their eccentricity and colourful escapades. Two of those I remember from my childhood were Victor and Mary M.

Victor was a tall, fierce-looking, moustachioed character who would ride around the village on his bike, peddling furiously as if undertaking some desperate secret mission. He wore a cape and wellington boots and lived independently in a small cottage. Rumour had it that he was injured by shrapnel during the war; no doubt, had Victor been alive today, he would have been diagnosed as suffering from post-traumatic stress disorder, and treated with empathy rather than mild amusement.

Mary M was a Punch-and-Judy lookalike character with a pointy chin and nose, and unkempt straggly hair tucked underneath a bonnet. Like Victor, she went everywhere on a bicycle, often pulling a cart or a child's pram behind her. She was a collector, a hoarder, and she would scour the countryside in search of coal, wood, and scrap which she used to take home with her, amassing a huge collection of junk at her bungalow home on Eagland Hill. Rumour had it that she was once caught by a policeman frantically riding her bicycle down the newly opened M6 motorway. But evidently Mary, who had a husband and four children, had the last laugh. For she was shrewd enough to know when she could make money from her many finds and wasn't averse to selling coal or scrap in exchange for a bob or two.

9

'Another Brick in the Wall' or the Top Class at Primary School

My life took a dramatic turn for the worse when I moved from Mrs Mitchell's class to the top class, where our teacher was Mr Shelley, the head teacher. Mr Shelley was a loud, bellowing, ferocious-looking character with a shock of red hair and a temper to match; he always wore a scruffy cream jacket. Rumour had it that he never actually qualified as a teacher but that his wartime service in schools had been enough to secure his future at Pilling CE School. Whether this is true or not, there is no doubt that he terrified many of his young charges. In today's climate he would have faced disciplinary charges for bullying, but in the sixties, without the stern scrutiny of Ofsted, anti-bullying legislation, and a battalion of child-protection officers, his behaviour went unchallenged.

I don't remember Mr Shelley ever striking out at a child, though he may well have done. No, he was too canny for that; his form of bullying was of the insidious, cruelly mocking kind that wrung out your insides, bleeding you dry of confidence. He favoured the bright kids, targeting the weak, the timid, or those he perceived as social misfits.

There was one boy in particular who bore the brunt of Mr Shelley's venom. Cheeky-faced, mischievous, scruffily dressed, with a perpetually runny nose, Billy Jones was frequently picked on, ritually humiliated by Mr Shelley, yet somehow escaped unscathed, showing amazing resilience and a refusal to be cowed. It's probably fair to say that his toughness came from being part of a large family where he was used to fighting his own battles.

Alas, I didn't have Billy's mettle during the many occasions Mr Shelley publicly abused me. He once mocked me for being slow and clumsy when I was trying to cut some paper and I couldn't get the blunt scissors to work properly.

'You stupid girl!' I can remember him bellowing at me in front of all my classmates. 'You're hopeless!' he roared, commanding some other unsuspecting classmate to take over, as I went hotter and redder, cowering like an injured puppy.

There was also the time he mocked me for the way I held my pen. Lurking in my memory is the notion that I was naturally left-handed as a child. For some reason, left-handedness was discouraged in those days. When I first started primary school at Preesall, my teachers, aided by my parents and grandparents, encouraged me to write with my right hand. This must have felt unnatural to me, because I have a peculiar way of holding my pen, clutching it between my index finger and middle finger, with my index finger curled over the pen and my thumb resting on the finger. Mr Shelley clearly found this unusual way of holding my pen a source of annoyance.

'Sit here,' he ordered, pointing at the desk in front of the classroom, in full view of thirty or so silenced classmates. 'Now, this is how you hold your pen, between finger and thumb, like this.' He proceeded to demonstrate the 'correct' way to hold a pen. 'I want you to write "I must hold my pen correctly" on every line until you have filled this page. And I don't want you to move until you have finished.'

Each desk came equipped with its own inkwell, but these were seldom used by my generation. Instead we relied on ink that came in small glass phials, labelled 'Quink'. The idea was that you dipped your pen into the phial and by squeezing a rubber suction tube you were able to refill your pen with new ink. Perhaps not surprisingly leaks were inevitable, splotches of thick bluey-black fluid landing indiscriminately, leaving an indelible trail over exercise books, desks, hands – not to mention school clothes! Writing was, indeed, a messy affair, and the only solution was to repair to the school toilets and come back armed with a wodge of paper towels to try to mop up the mess. It was only as we reached the end of primary school that the cartridge pen, a neater, supposedly cleaner version of the fountain pen, made its foray into the classroom. But even then, the plastic cartridges that neatly encased the ink had a habit of leaking.

The indignity of having to sit in front of the class was nothing compared to the ignominy I suffered when I was part of the school handbell team. The handbell team was Mr Shelley's pride and joy, formed of pupils from the top class. Each ringer was assigned a bell; the bigger boys tended to be entrusted with the heavier bells and the girls with the lightweight ones. During practice sessions, we were ordered to stand in a line, the big bells at one end and the smaller ones at the other.

Naturally, Mr Shelley enjoyed the sense of self-importance attached to being a conductor. As he pointed his baton – or, more accurately, a ruler – towards us ringers, we were required to respond with the quick flick of the wrist that would send our bells tinkling across the airwaves. From endless rehearsals, we managed to build a passable repertoire of harmonious ring-a-ling tunes ranging from 'Frère Jacques' to 'Three Blind Mice.' Over time, the school handbell team built up a following locally, entertaining at older people's concerts and community gatherings.

Being picked for the handbell team demanded speed, precision and good coordination. These were qualities that I woefully lacked, though in reality it was probably confidence that failed me. Mr Shelley frequently became exasperated when any child failed to ring a bell on time, bellowing louder at each mistimed attempt.

Our sessions went something like this:

'Right, let's start with "Do-Re-Mi"' Mr Shelley commanded, baton poised with all the aplomb of Sir Malcolm Sargent.

Off we'd go, Mr Shelley jabbing his baton towards each of his musical protégés, arms swinging from one side of the room to the other, sending sharp staccato prods in the direction of each bell-ringer, cream jacket flapping wildly, eyes glowering menacingly, moving about like a dancing dervish.

It only took one mistimed bell-ring to fuel his frustration. 'No, No, that's not right!' he'd scream as he ran his hands through this red hair, face getting even redder. 'Let's try again, and this time I don't want any mistakes.'

This left me quaking with fear, dreading the moment he thrust his ruler in my direction, in case I made a mistake. It turned out to be a self-fulfilling prophecy after I failed to ring the bell at the right moment during the playing of 'Frère Jacques' and threw the whole musical sequence out of synch. My mistiming was down to pure terror; when Mr Shelley pointed his baton towards me I simply froze. Perversely, I was so anxious about not getting it wrong, I ended up doing exactly that.

'Get out, you silly chump!' he thundered ('silly chump' was one of his favourite expressions). 'And don't bother coming back.' Hot-faced, I retreated tearfully, a shivering wreck, humiliated and sickened. It didn't help matters that almost the entire class was a member of the handbell team, leaving me with an even greater sense of isolation and failure. Mr Shelley's intimidation created a legacy of fear of being publicly humiliated. To this day, I remain fearful of doing anything that requires any kind of practical skills in front of others, in case it makes me look awkward or clumsy. The ghost of Mr Shelley has haunted me many times during my career, albeit in different guises: the intimidating female NHS manager; the voluntary-sector control freak who sought to belittle staff in order to bolster his own power; and, more latterly, the charity manager whose undermining behaviour was anything but charitable. Now, older and wiser, I'm determined that if he appears in my life again, I'll be waiting.

Back then teachers were authority figures, people to be respected and revered. Like many of my generation, I was taught by my parents to show respect to adults. That meant using the title Mr or Mrs, never referring to them by their Christian names. It wouldn't have entered my head to challenge Mr Shelley or complain to my parents. They were also of the generation who were in awe of teachers, policemen, and doctors, bowing down to their perceived status and authority. Unlike some parents of today, who stampede in to the head teacher's office at the slightest perceived injustice, it would never have occurred to my parents to question this authority. Who would have thought being grounded for texting on your mobile phone could trigger a crisis of world-war proportions between your parents and head teacher?

There was one memorable occasion when Mr Shelley met his own hubris after being given a very public dose of humiliation by none other than his wife. It happened as we ate our lunch in the school dining room. The door opened and Mrs Shelley flew in.

'Jones! It's you, Jones!' she roared at Mrs Jones, a young, newly qualified supply teacher who had been quietly tucking in to her beef stew at the teachers' table. Her fingers waved menacingly as Mrs Jones visibly cowered, her eyes downcast.

Mr Shelley stumbled to his feet, his face beetroot-red and awash with horror, and manfully ejected his wife from the room, shoving her shoulder with his raised right arm. There was a stunned, collective silence as the entire school – all ninety or so pupils – watched this drama play out before our eyes with a mixture of fascination and amusement. I would have been about nine or ten at the time, too young to fully understand the facts of life, but old enough to recognise that Mr Shelley's marital fidelity was being called into question. Soon the whole school, the parents and community, were all buzzing with the news of Mr Shelley's 'affair' with the supply teacher. Soon after this, Mrs Shelley disappeared from the adjoining school house, where she lived with her husband, never to be seen in school again.

After that, things carried on pretty much as normal. By today's standards, Mr Shelley was a very poor teacher, and we learnt very little. As this was in the in pre- national curriculum days, teachers were given a free rein over teaching content and lesson planning. There's no doubt that many teachers were driven by a strong instinct to provide each and every one of their pupils with a rounded education – Mrs Mitchell was one of these – but Mr Shelley's philosophy of education left a lot to be desired.

Formal lessons, such as maths and English, were virtually non-existent. Typically, an English lesson would consist of copying a page of text from a book in our best handwriting. A maths lesson would take the form of a game of 'shopkeeper' with Mr Shelley's desk becoming a makeshift shop stacked with cereal cartons, tins, jars and chocolate wrappers. Each of us would take it in turn to be the shopkeeper, responsible for handling cash, while the rest of the class made their purchases. I enjoyed playing shopkeeper, but though it taught me the basic rudiments of adding up, it didn't teach me anything about multiplication, division, fractions and percentages, and left me feeling woefully inadequate when I started secondary school maths classes.

During our so-called geography lessons, Mr Shelley devised a game where we would measure and record a mile in distance from school. To do this, we had to pace the distance from the school gates to Fluke Hall, where the mile ended. It was an enjoyable way to spend a sunny September afternoon, and no doubt had *some* educational value, but it taught us very little about the wider world of countries and continents that existed beyond the cosy confines of Pilling. If our formal lessons were sparse in knowledge, then our physical education lessons were plentiful. PE consisted of endless games of rounders; there was hardly a day went by that we didn't play rounders. But Mr Shelley's imagination failed to stretch beyond this to the host of other opportunities that could have been offered to us ... I don't remember any of us being taught gymnastics, dance, netball or football.

To encourage learning and 'good' behaviour, Mr Shelley created a graduate system, as an incentive for us to work hard. Pupils who produced consistently good work or behaved well in class could earn themselves the title of 'graduate.' As graduate you were entitled to many privileges, including being allowed to write in red ink! You could also take responsibility for answering the school telephone (with no school secretary or receptionist, all calls came directly to the head teacher's classroom), and claim your own allotment space in the school garden. I can remember feeling thrilled when I was awarded 'graduate' status and couldn't wait to race home to tell my parents the news.

The school had a head boy and girl, who were both in the top class. The head boy was Keith Norris, that shy boy from Manchester who'd joined Mrs Mitchell's class as a new starter on the same day as me. The head girl was Jenny Catterall, a farmer's daughter whose eleven-plus success secured her a place at Fleetwood Grammar School, followed by a career of her own in teaching.

One of my friends was a shy, studious girl. I'll call her Pauline. She was the only child of a neurotic mother who was overprotective and driven by irrational fears that her daughter would be taken away from her by a terrible illness or accident. To counter this, she used every conceivable measure to ensure Pauline was protected from harm. To ward off illness or infection, Pauline was required to wear three or four cardigans, buttoned up high, to school. She wasn't allowed to go out to play, and her home became a shrine to books and learning. The result of this cosseting was that she grew up to be fiercely intelligent and knowledgeable, but emotionally and socially stifled and crushed. When she later had the opportunity to escape the cloistered confines of her home life, she did so with spectacular results: soon after leaving school at sixteen she went on holiday, met a man, and ran away from home to live with him, in a desperate bid for independence.

Among my memories of schooldays are the smells of cooked cabbage emanating from the kitchen, mingled with the disinfectant smells of cleaning fluids. The school cook, Lilian Warbreck, was good at whisking up fine, wholesome meals. These typically comprised roast beef or pork, or stew, which was always stringy, mashed potatoes and vegetables, including the ubiquitous watery cabbage. Puddings were on an unvarying theme of jam roly-poly or spotted dick served with lashings of thin, pale custard. But the food was always piping hot and fresh and it was always cooked from scratch; there were no short cuts with Mrs Warbreck.

During break time, while the lads played football using the two former air-raid shelters as goals, we girls would play on the climbing frames. These were metal frames of the kind commonly seen today in parks and public playgrounds. We would perform acrobatic feats, dangling from the top bars, hanging upside down, body weight suspended mid-air, knickers on full show. We were oblivious to any notions of sexual impropriety; we were that naïve.

The trick was to climb up to the top bar (about six feet from the ground), sit on it and gradually lower the upper part of the body, until you were suspended upside down from the knee, with head and arms facing towards the ground. The braver ones among us would wrap our feet around the bar and our entire body weight would be suspended from the top of the foot curled around the bar, just below the ankles. I still shudder with horror to think how one crucial slip could have sent us plunging head first to the concrete below, and to possible paralysis. Health and safety was clearly not as high on the agenda in schools as it is today.

10

Doctors, Dentists and an Encounter With Death

Back in those days, childhood ailments and illnesses were treated with due reverence and respect. Appendicitis nearly always led to the removal of the appendix – an appendectomy – and it seemed to be quite common at our school. The operation meant a lengthy stay in hospital, followed by an even longer stay away from school. I can remember several children in our school being absent from school for what seemed an inordinately long time after appendix operations. They had to stay in hospital for about a week, followed by something like two weeks' recuperation at home, meaning three glorious weeks off school! When they returned to school, pale-faced and delicate, they were treated like royalty, with the other children warned against being 'too rough' around them.

Having your tonsils removed was also a major clinical procedure, requiring a two-day stay in hospital and a fortnight off school. In those days tonsillectomy operations were carried out with routine regularity. My brother was one of those who fell victim to the surgeon's scalpel after suffering from persistent colds and sore throats. But the nice thing about this operation was that you were encouraged to eat lots of jelly and ice cream in order to soothe the soreness. That made the whole thing a lot more palatable for my brother and a whole generation of

spend a day off school. And if your mum was kind, as mine was, you were rewarded with the latest edition of *Bunty* to read.

Away from school, I enjoyed happy days playing on the farm with Anne Rossall, or playing at home with my brother. Living next door to the parish church, St John's, we befriended the sexton (an officer of the church), a kindly but eccentric bachelor called Tom Butler, who used to tend to the church grounds and was a familiar figure in the village, riding around on his bicycle. It was through Tom that we developed a morbid fascination with graves. One of our favourite games was 'graveyards.' We earmarked a plot of garden as a graveyard and dug out burial plots for each of my dolls. Our mother was horrified.

'Why don't you play something else?' she suggested helpfully.

'Why, what's wrong with playing graveyards?' I countered defiantly.

'Because it's not very nice,' she responded, without elaborating.

Eventually, she banned us from playing this macabre game but without explaining the sensitivities of death. It left us feeling puzzled, though at that point death hadn't really touched our lives.

The shooting of black civil rights leader Martin Luther King in April 1968, followed a few months later by the assassination of American senator 'Bobby' Kennedy in the June, were the first occasions I became aware of the brutal reality of death.

Newspapers were plastered with photos of the blond, good-looking Bobby, along with graphic accounts of him being shot as he took part in the American presidential election campaign in Los Angeles. There was extensive television coverage of the tragedy and commentators were plunged into a frenzy of debate.

Death entered my own life in a horrifying way a short time later, though it wasn't a human death but an animal death that left an indelible mark on my psyche. My friend, Anne Rossall, had an adorable black poodle which she called Susan. She became my surrogate dog in the absence of a pet of my own. One afternoon, after we'd arrived home from school, I went across the road to play with Anne on the farm. We were met at the gate by an ashen-faced Hilda, her eyes smudged from crying.

'Susan's been killed,' she announced, immediately breaking down in to sobs. We were incredulous; Hilda explained to us that the dog had escaped from the house, darted across the road and was hit by a bus. She was killed immediately.

Seeing our wide-eyed stares, Hilda decided to show us the poor animal. Why she chose to shock us in this way, I'll never know, but I think she may been acting from a misguided belief that by letting us see the body we would be able to accept the finality of Susan's fate. Whatever the reason, the sight of the poor poodle, her head lolling and mouth gaping open, a grotesque parody of a smile on her gleaming white teeth, eyes fixed in horror as she lay supine in Hilda's arms, is one I'll never forget. It was a harsh lesson in the realities of life and death, and a world away from my childhood game of graveyards.

After Susan's death, heartbroken Hilda and Bob decided to give the dog a good send off, organising the canine equivalent of a funeral on the farm. Bob, Hilda and Anne, together with Hilda's mother, all dressed in solemn black, and a plot was chosen for the burial at the bottom of the garden. Hilda thinks I must have been present at the funeral but I don't remember it. Susan was eventually replaced by another dog, an adorable puppy called Cindy – another poodle, naturally.

11

'We're All Going on a Summer Holiday'

In the sixties, Blackpool faced competition from the new package-holiday industry, offering people the opportunity to taste a wider world beyond Britain's breezy shores. My grandma was seduced by advertisements promising the allure and glamour of exotic destinations like Spain and Majorca. She and her friends, Joan Crook and Nell Cooper, became part of the new 'jet set', jetting off to Palma Nova, Majorca. They came back buzzing with excitement, unable to stop talking about their dream holiday in Majorca, but mispronouncing its name, blissfully ignorant of the idioms of the Spanish language that rendered the 'j' phonetic linguistically redundant.

'Oh, we had a wonderful time in Majorca – lovely beaches, lots of sunshine, and the Spanish people were so nice,' trilled Grandma in her affected Mayoress's voice, as she produced yet another photo of what appeared to be the same sun-drenched beach.

If Majorca was magical, then imagine the wider world of possibilities that soon opened up as package holidays flourished – the Greek Islands, Cyprus, Portugal, France!

Grandma wasn't the only one bitten by the foreign-holiday bug. When Uncle Jack Wright and Auntie Lizzie went to Canada for three weeks, we never heard the end of it. Uncle Jack, a keen photographer, installed a screen and slideshow projector in his best room and inflicted on us an epic show of his holiday slides. We were forced us to endure hours of imprisonment in a darkened room, viewing Lake Ontario from a thousand-and-one different perspectives to the accompaniment of his dull monotone voice, as he squinted myopically through his thick bifocals (he had very poor eyesight which led to his eventual blindness), pausing interminably over each slide.

Closer to home, Granny and Grandad hopped on the short flight from Blackpool Airport to Jersey. I can remember going with my mum and dad to the airport to wave them off. Back then, there was a certain cachet to flying; you would have thought Granny, in her smart pale-blue jersey two-piece, and Grandad, in his best checked sports jacket, were Elizabeth Taylor and Richard Burton as we watched them go through the departure gates to fly away to what was, to our childhood minds, the equivalent of the South Pacific Islands.

Fast forward to the present day and Blackpool Airport has closed its doors to the last passenger aircraft. It's a sad day for Blackpool and for local people who loved the convenience of having an airport on their doorstep and being able to hop on to a Ryanair or Jet2 flight to sunnier climes.

Back then, all of our family was in awe of aeroplanes; we were captivated by the excitement of this new jet era. Sometimes we would venture to Manchester Airport and decamp on the observation terrace just to watch all the mighty Boeing 707s taking off and landing. One day, feeling intrepid, my mum decided to treat us to a 'pleasure flight' on one of the airport's smaller commercial aircraft. Dad refused to fly, insisting on keeping his feet firmly on the ground while Mum, my brother and I circled over Manchester Airport at a great height, overwhelmed by the dizzying sensation of lurching over fields at distorted angles and seeing houses in miniature. After twenty minutes in the air, we landed breathless with excitement, desperate to tell our friends that we'd been in a real aeroplane! Of course, today we wouldn't think twice about hopping on a plane to soak up the Mediterranean sunshine or even venturing on a long-haul trip to the deepest jungles of South America, but back in the sixties flying was a real novelty.

Our family holidays were few and far between, mainly because my dad hated going away anywhere. One year he relented and we went to Butlins in Pwllheli. I would have been about eight, and my brother six, at the time. As holidays go, it was a true *Hi-de-Hi!* experience, with 'Morning, campers!' style greetings blaring out from the tannoy religiously at seven o'clock each morning, a clarion call to rise and shine and get ready for the day's packed programme of entertainment.

Meals were served on long tables, military-style, in a dining room packed with five hundred hungry holidaymakers, with the clattering of cutlery and crockery drowning out all conversation. The food was unappetising fare – stringy beef stew; cold lumpy potatoes; thick, steamed puddings – served from giant vats, and tasting not dissimilar to school dinners.

In an exhausting programme of entertainment, we could take our pick from a dizzying array of different activities, from tenpin bowling and tiddlywinks contests, to roller-coaster rides, picnics on the beach, donkey rides, amusement arcades and ice skating. We enjoyed the thrill of the impressive chairlift, with its commanding views of the beach and coastline.

In the evening the fun continued unabated, with ballroom dancing, talent contests and the Miss Butlins beauty pageants, all presented by the famous Butlins Redcoats in their trademark jaunty red jackets. To my embarrassment, my mum entered me for the Miss Junior Butlins contest, and I remember wishing I could melt away as I blushingly shuffled across the stage, shoulders rounded, eyes averted from the gaze of the spotlight.

Closer to home, we sometimes popped in to the Forton motorway service station – or 'Top Rank' as we called it – for tea. This was one of the earliest service stations, launched after the M6 motorway opened in 1965 cutting through a swathe of Lancashire countryside to create a vital transport artery between London and Scotland. Forton Service Station, with its iconic hexagonal Pennine Tower and disc-shaped top-floor restaurant and viewing platform, was considered to be at the cutting edge of iconic sixties modern architecture when it first opened.

Today, to my mind, it looks out of place, a faded relic long past its prime. But back in the sixties, it was *the* place to be. On Sunday evenings we used to drive there and tuck in to a meal of fish and chips with bread and butter in the spacious ground-floor canteen, watching the traffic zipping up and down the motorway. It felt exciting and novel back then, though no doubt today's generation would baulk at the idea of dining out for the evening in what was, in essence, a posher version of a greasy transport cafe.

Occasionally, we'd go up in the lift to the top of the tower to look at the views from the public viewing platform and marvel at the panoramic vistas across Morecambe Bay and the Fylde Coast. We'd sneak a look through the windows at the restaurant perched atop the tower, but we never dined there; it was too expensive for our pockets. The tower closed to the public in 1989 due to health and safety regulations.

To exit the service station, we used to drive through the 'trade' entrance. Officially, this route was out of bounds to motorists, so we were always watchful for prying police officers. The alternative would have meant driving along the motorway to the next junction. It gave our outings an extra thrill, knowing we were doing something illicit!

12

Thunderbirds Are Go!

The advent of colour television in 1967 brought a whole new, exciting dimension to the lives of children across the nation, and my brother and I were no exception. *Blue Peter*, *Crackerjack*, and *Thunderbirds* were among our favourite programmes. *Thunderbirds* thrilled us as we watched the exploits of International Rescue, headed by the heroic Tracy family, captains of a mighty fleet of rockets and spaceships, and not forgetting Brains, sassy Lady Penelope, her faithful chauffeur Parker, and the villainous Hood. Geoff and I were both terrified by Hood and cowered behind the sofa each time he transfixed his captors with his menacing hypnotic eyes.

Watching *Dr Who* had the same effect on us. Each time the Daleks made their entrance, with their flashing lights and strange voices proclaiming nasally, 'We are the Daleks! Exterminate! Exterminate!' we would retreat in fright and hide behind the sofa. One day Mum declared that *Dr Who* was for grown-ups and forbade us to watch it.

With *Blue Peter* we were on safer territory: the avuncular John Noakes and Christopher Trace, and Brown Owl-ish Valerie Singleton, opened up a whole world of learning and discovery. They were welcomed as friends in to our home twice each week, Mondays and Thursdays, just before tea. *Crackerjack* was enjoyable for different reasons: Friday night was *Crackerjack* night, which meant no school the next day. But no sooner had you said '*Crackerjack* pencil' than it was Monday morning and school again, for weekends always flew by.

The Beverley Hillbillies was another programme we liked to watch. The series centred on the escapades of the hapless and naïve Clampett family who find their fortune and become overnight millionaires after discovering oil on their land. It was much loved by adults and children alike, and nowhere more so than in our house. Feisty battleaxe Granny Clampett, docile Jed Clampett, gormless Jethro, ditzy Ellie May and greedy banker Mr Drysdale were larger-than-life characters, and we looked forward to watching their antics.

Once a week we were allowed to stay up to watch *The Man from U.N.C.L.E.* featuring agents Napoleon Solo (Robert Vaughn) and Illya Kuryakin (David McCallum). It was Illya Kuryakin who gave me my first schoolgirl crush. I was captivated by his sexy smile and blond floppy locks. Real boys were still a world away, but in debonair Illya Kuryakin I'd discovered a handsome hero whom I could secretly ogle from the safety of my front living room. I suppose I would have been about nine or ten at the time.

My mother used to take us on the bus to Blackpool to see the 'pictures'. One of my favourite films was *Whistle Down the Wind*, starring Alan Bates as an escaped convict who seeks refuge on a farm and convinces the local children that he is Jesus. It was made in Lancashire, with scenes filmed in the pretty village of Downham, in the Ribble Valley. It features Hayley Mills as one of the children who is in thrall to 'Jesus'. The film offers a wonderful commentary on childhood innocence, trust and loss in an era when children were less exposed to cynicism. The producers recruited local child actors. One of them, Diane Holgate, who played the role of farm child Nan Bostock, came to Pilling School to open a school fete, much to our delight.

Books also formed a big part of my childhood; I inherited a love of reading from my mother, who was a prolific reader, as was her mother, my grandma. Not surprisingly, as a pony lover, my favourite book was *Black Beauty*, but I also enjoyed reading the novels of Enid Blyton, in particular the *Malory Towers* adventures. I was captivated by the tales of this fictional girls' boarding school in Cornwall, and the exploits of heroine Darrell Rivers and classmates – the sharp-tongued Alica, timid Mary-Lou and spoilt brat, Gwendoline. Anne Rossall and I used to read the stories aloud to each other; sprawled across the bed as we munched chocolate, we would plot how we could swap our humdrum life at Pilling School for the impossible glamour of boarding school.

When I was around nine, I decided to write a letter to the Prime Minister, Harold Wilson. I'm not sure what prompted this, as I'd never shown any interest in politics – or current affairs of any kind, for that matter. Innocently, I wrote a nice letter to the premier saying I'd seen him on the television and wanted to wish him well in office. I was thrilled when an envelope arrived in the post bearing the official postmark of 10 Downing Street. Inside was a letter from Harold Wilson's secretary, thanking me for my good wishes, together with a personally signed photograph from the great man and his wife. Sadly, although I kept this for many years, I have no idea what happened to it. It may well still be languishing in a cupboard or a drawer at my childhood home, for all I know.

13

'Bad Moon Rising'

Mr Shelley's bullying aside, it's probably fair to say I had a charmed childhood. However, as I approached my eleventh birthday, the soft, petal-strewn garden of childhood began to yield to the first prickly brambles of adolescence. Among the precursors to the harsher realities of growing up were the start of my periods and the impending eleven-plus exam that would determine my entire future.

With my general education at Pilling CE School woefully lacking, it was hardly surprising that sex education didn't get a look in. In fairness to Mr Shelley, there was no expectation on schools to teach any form of sex or reproductive education. Despite the sexual revolution in the sixties, schools were surprisingly backward in teaching this subject, due to misguided notions about the loss of childhood innocence. What little I learnt about the 'facts of life', I picked up from playground whispers and sniggers – there were vague mutterings about boys putting their 'willies inside girls' holes' to make babies. I found the whole idea disgusting and distasteful.

When I was about ten, my mum tried to prepare me for menstruation, gently explaining to me that girls start to bleed in readiness for the time they have babies. I didn't really understand the connection between blood and babies, but it was just as well my mother had forewarned me – because when I was ten I started my periods, and was the first of my friends to do so. Despite my mum's pep talk, there still lurked within me the awful thought that I had caught some dread disease and it was with trepidation that I plucked up the courage to tell her of my discovery. Her response was totally unexpected.

'Right, we're going to go to Blackpool and I'm going to buy you a nice new dress,' she said as she pulled me towards her and gave me a hug.

'What's that for?' I asked, totally nonplussed.

'Because you're on the way to becoming a grown woman. It's something to celebrate!'

So off we trudged on the number 85 bus to Blackpool on a girly afternoon, and I was allowed to choose my own dress. I can remember going into Paige's, on the corner of Abingdon Street and Church Street, and picking a turquoise dress with pink candy stripes and puffed sleeves, and an elasticated frill at the wrist. I felt I'd grown up by ten years! My new dress helped to take away some of the trauma and humiliation at the prospect of a lifetime of periods and bothersome sanitary wear. After that, we went to the Yorkshire Fisheries, on Topping Street, and I was treated to fish and chips.

It's when looking back that I can value my mum's approach to menstruation. Her idea of celebrating an important rite of passage with a new dress was a loving and life-affirming gesture that still holds a special place in my heart to this day. Many years later, working as a health promotion specialist and delivering sex education sessions to parents in order to help them become educators of their own children, I used my mum's example to illustrate how incorporating a sense of celebration into growing up and adolescent development could remove some of the fear associated with puberty. I like to think it helped, in my case.

Throughout my last year at primary school, we were continually reminded of the looming eleven-plus exam by Mr Shelley, by our parents, and by our peers. It dogged us as a nagging presence, like toothache. The messages were clear: the eleven-plus was an important milestone; it determined your future education and, with that, your life and career chances. Pass this test and you were practically guaranteed a gilded future at the grammar school, and a glittering career. Fail, and you were destined for a second-rate education at secondary modern school, and a lowly jobs market.

Mr Shelley, for all his faults as a teacher, refused to entertain failure, seeing it as a reflection on his capabilities as a head teacher. Hell-bent on getting results, he ensured our last six months of primary school were devoted to a feverish round of mock eleven-plus papers. What Mr Shelley didn't realise was that no matter how many mock exams we took, they could never compensate for the gaping holes in our general education over the two years we'd been in his class. It was like baking a cake: it was no good putting fancy icing on top of a fruit cake that lacked sufficient dried fruit to give it moisture, substance and taste.

To stretch this metaphor a bit further, the proof of the pudding was in the eating: in a class of about twenty-five, as far as I can remember, only two children passed the exam and were rewarded with a coveted place at Fleetwood Grammar School.

On the day of the eleven-plus exam, in 1968, I was stupendously nervous, a quivering wreck. My parents had high expectations of me passing and gaining a prized place at grammar school. But after what seemed like hours of ploughing my way through a series of mind-boggling mental gymnastics, I came away feeling sick with apprehension. I knew there was no way I would have passed. I'd spent too long pondering over each question and failed to answer them all.

Afterwards, my mother took me to Lancaster on the bus as a treat. She bought me a Spidograph from the Rocking Horse toy shop, on New Street, as a reward for working hard. A Spidograph was a geometric drawing device, with a series of discs and wheels which enabled you to draw lots of interesting patterns and shapes. It was the must-have toy back in 1968, yet I could barely bring myself to open the box, feeling I'd done little to warrant it.

Looking back, I'm not sure I can in all honesty put my eleven-plus failure down to my abysmal education. Perhaps I don't have the capacity for reasoning and logic that some of the sections seem to demand. Recently, one of the Sunday supplements featured a mock eleven-plus exam paper, and I found myself completely flummoxed by some of questions. Go on: try for yourself!

Test One

Change the first word of the third pair in the same way as the other pairs to give a new word.

Example: bind, hind bare, hare but, hut

1. quiz, quite flux, flute plan …
2. practice, price stopping, sting pleasant …
3. pat, pout flat, flout rat …
4. sludge, slug fudge, fug budge …
5. frame, blame fright, blight frown …

Test Two

From the information supplied, answer the questions.

-   Naomi, Fern, Husna, and Deborah are friends at secondary school.
-   Fern, Naomi and Husna learn Spanish. Naomi, Husna and Deborah study art.
-   Husna learns Greek. Deborah and Naomi do textiles.
-   Husna, Fern and Deborah study French. Deborah, Fern and Naomi do chemistry.
-   Fern and Deborah do geography. Fern and Husna do music.

1. Who does French but does not do art?
2. Who does chemistry but not geography?
3. Who does art and Spanish but does not do geography and textiles?
4. Who does not study music, Greek or Spanish?
5. Who does the fewest subjects?

*Questions taken from the Bond Series of *11 plus 10 minute Test Papers(Oxford)*.

Be honest: how quickly did it take you to reach the answers? A *Crackerjack* pencil if you managed to get the answers in under five minutes. Alas, I struggled. Perhaps I never was grammar school material, after all!

One spring morning in 1968, Mr Shelley came to see my parents. He broke the news to them that I'd failed, timing his visit before the official announcement of the eleven-plus results. To be fair to Mr Shelley, he was acting in my best interests. He knew how disappointed I would be and he wanted my parents to consider other options. He pointed out that there was a very good independent school for girls in Blackpool – Elmslie School. They had an entrance exam, which I would have to pass, but I would receive an excellent education (when my parents told me this later, the irony did not escape me).

After my parents gently relayed to me the news that I'd failed, I wasn't in the least surprised; in my heart, I knew I hadn't answered enough questions to warrant a pass.

'You did your best,' my mum offered as solace. 'And that's all that matters.' I wasn't convinced; clearly, in this case, my best wasn't good enough, my critical inner voice told me. It was this critical inner voice that drove me to become a high achiever later in life, driven to succeed academically when I became a mature student, determined that I would never again court failure.

'How would you like to take the entrance exam for Elmslie?'

Mum asked me. But I'd seen the purple blazers; I'd seen the superior-looking gaggles of girls strutting along the Blackpool streets in their Elmslie colours; I wanted to go somewhere where there'd be *boys* as well. I was pubescent; I'd had my first period! I'd already made my mind up: I was going to St Aidan's Church of England School, Preesall. I was going to be a secondary modern kid!

14

'Those Were the Days'

In 1968, demure, dimpled blonde teenager Mary Hopkin had a number-one hit with 'Those were the Days', a winsome folk song reminiscing on the days 'we thought would never end' after winning the TV talent show *Opportunity Knocks*. In the same year, I started secondary school, and it's fair to say that the words of this song have a great deal of resonance, for I count my days at St Aidan's as among the best in my life.

St Aidan's Church of England School was an archetypal secondary school. It opened 1963 with just one hundred and sixty-eight pupils and eleven staff, after being built to serve the needs of the expanding rural population of the six Over Wyre parishes – Knott End, Preesall, Stalmine, Hambleton, Pilling and Out Rawcliffe. By the time I started in September 1968, the number of pupils had risen to two hundred and forty, with fourteen staff. Today the school has almost tripled in size, boasting nearly seven hundred students from all across the Fylde Coast. The head teacher and deputy head are part of a management team of six, and there are around fifty teachers and teaching assistants.

My first day at St Aidan's was memorable because we nearly didn't make it after the school bus broke down. I can remember standing at the bus stop, a quivering nervous wreck, with my mum and a handful of other new starters waiting for a single-decker bus that never arrived. Minutes ticked by and still no sign.

As the fingers of the clock crept ever nearer to nine o'clock, I found myself feeling sick with anxiety about being late on my first day. My mum decided to take action. She knocked on the door of our friends and neighbours, Bob and Hilda Rossall, to ask if they would mind taking us to school in their car. Their daughter, Anne, who was by now in her second year at secondary school and something of an old hand, was also in the bus queue. Bob duly arrived at the bus stop in his Ford Zodiac and we all piled in. By the time we reached the school gates, it was nearly half past nine. Our late arrival meant we'd missed the morning assembly, so we were escorted directly to our form rooms.

I was assigned a place in Form 1M. My form teacher was Mr Maund, a young, energetic English teacher, straight from teacher training college and as nervous and fresh around the gills as his young charges. Mr Maund was bespectacled, with dark hair neatly Brylcreemed in place and he sported a small moustache – and a look of earnestness. He wore a pristine white shirt and shiny black shoes, and he was clearly keen to make an impression. To our eleven-year-old eyes, he looked old, as all teachers do. But in truth he was probably little more than twenty-one years old.

Among my fellow classmates there were many I recognised from Pilling School, including that shy young boy who had been a new starter on the same day as me at primary school, Keith Norris. But there were lots of children in my class I didn't know. We were all like little sugar bags fizzing with unspent energy, bursting to break free from the stiff collars of our new uniforms and the strange rules and hierarchies that signified secondary school and spelt out our lowly status. Perhaps not surprisingly, we felt restless, fidgety, edgy, as we sat in our form room on that first day, listening as Mr Maund instructed us on the importance of backing all our exercise books with paper – either plain brown paper or something a little bit more decorative – in order to protect them from daily wear and tear.

Looking back, we were very lucky to have him as our form tutor, for as we all settled in – he as well as us – we found ourselves benefiting greatly from his devoted care. His kindness, approachability and gentle humour were the antithesis of Mr Shelley's harsh regime. And I like to think a special bond was forged during those months that remains to this day.

In those days, the St Aidan's uniform consisted of a grey V-necked sweater edged with maroon piping around the neckline, grey wool pleated skirt, grey or white blouse and a maroon-and-grey tie. Grey knee-high wool socks and unflattering grey wool knickers completed the ensemble. The latter were seen as an important component of the PE uniform, which also included a red T-shirt, skimpy grey pleated skirt, and black plimsolls. Having regulation grey knickers meant that if your skirt rode up during netball – as it often did - and you revealed more than you intended, then at least you were still adhering to school uniform!

Before starting secondary school, I went with my mum on the number 85 bus to Blackpool to get kitted out with my uniform from Rawcliffe's, the school outfitters, on Birley Street. Among the items on our shopping list was the obligatory school satchel. I plumped for a cumbersome, orangey-brown bag with a thick shoulder strap in taut, unyielding leather. It had several capacious compartments for carrying books and pencils, and it weighed a ton. It was paid for, I think, by my granny and grandad.

My swanky new satchel must have cost them a fortune, but it stood the test of time, surviving all my school years, even though it was battered and worn by the end of the fifth year and bore inscriptions relating to several 'boyfriends' and pop stars, indelibly etched with compass point and biro – 'I luv Bill xxx', 'Donny Osmond forever xxx', 'Man U. champs.' Within days of starting secondary school, my satchel was swiftly put to its purpose, soon bulging with thick textbooks and exercise books collected from each subject teacher. And with lessons in close on a dozen different subjects, it's little wonder I felt lopsided, weighed down by the sheer burden of carrying half a hundredweight of books as I trudged from one classroom to another.

Today, as I watch children ambling to St Aidan's I'm astounded at how much school uniforms have changed. Girl 'students' today (not pupils, as we were then) wear bright maroon jumpers over grey-and-white striped blouses, their necks no longer constrained by having to wear a tie. The boys have a choice of traditional collar and tie or a summer polo-necked T-shirt. Girls can wear grey skirts or trousers, though most seem to wear skirts.

But what surprises me most is that you rarely see children carrying traditional satchels any more. Today's students seem to favour canvas holdalls, backpacks or rucksacks slung casually over their shoulder, although apparently the leather bag is making a comeback as a must-have accessory, in a range of colours including pink and cream. Haute couture, it seems, has hit high school. And it amazes me to learn that many of today's computer-confident youngsters have their own iPads on which to store all their information, which means they no longer have to lug a library's worth of books around with them.

In my day, there were strict rules concerning uniform: no make-up, no jewellery, no trousers, no short skirts, i.e. more than three inches above the knee (girls); and for the boys, no hair worn below the collar. Clearly, we girls fared less favourably than the lads when it came to uniform. Later, as we grew in confidence and became more school-savvy, we'd roll the waistband of our skirts up to make them look shorter, turning ourselves into mini Michelin girls, with bulging midriffs.

Boys were forced to endure hair inspections in order to check hair-length rules were being adhered to. These were carried out with clockwork regularity by one of the senior teachers – usually

Mr Gledhill – and they took place as we all lined up in the school yard, prior to going to lessons. Mr Gledhill, as befitted his status as head of boys' PE and careers, was slender and wiry. He wasn't tall but he carried himself erectly, his shoulders back and chest puffed out with military authority. He wore his dark hair in a neat short back and sides, with a sharp side parting, and he expected the same high standards in his charges. He would stride down the boys' queue, carefully checking each boy's hair. Any lad deemed to be in contravention of the 'no hair below the collar' rule was given a sharp tap on the shoulder. Not a word was uttered, but the message was clear: go and get a haircut, or be prepared to face the consequences.

St Aidan's, perched prominently on the side of Preesall Hill, was visible for miles around thanks to its distinctive sixties turquoise facade. In 1968, the actual school building was probably half its current size. It consisted of a long T-shaped two-storey block of classrooms, forming the spinal column that still exists today. Located at one end was another smaller block of four classrooms. These included an upstairs science laboratory dominated by benches arranged in long rows; from each bench protruded a line of gas taps for powering the Bunsen burners. Next to the science lab was the school library, which also doubled up as a classroom. Below the science lab was the woodwork workshop, fitted with wooden workbenches and an assortment of lathes and joinery tools and all the paraphernalia for metalwork. Below the library was the domestic science room, with its gleaming cookers, fridges and spotless work surfaces, and leading off from this was a small carpeted alcove. This was designed to look and feel like the sort of dining room you might have at home; here pupils could practise the art of food service and presentation.

The main entrance hall and reception area were dominated by a central staircase and steps leading to the main corridors on the first and second storey of the main classroom block. To the right of the entrance hall was a passageway to the dining room and the main hall. This was the corridor of power, housing the head teacher's office and the school secretary's office on one side, and on the other side, the staffroom. The head teacher was Mr Peirse, and there will be more of him in a later chapter.

The school secretary, Mrs Rossall, was flinty-eyed with iron grey hair in neat curls and a brusque, officious manner. I think she must have missed her vocation in life, for she carried the air of authority of a teacher. If you ever needed to knock on the door of the school office for some change for your bus money, she would glower at you for having the effrontery to interrupt her work.

As it still is today, the main hall was dominated by a huge stage with an elegant backcloth and grey drapes running across the entire width. The school hall also doubled as a gymnasium, with its gleaming apparatus of wooden ladders and climbing frames affixed to the walls and climbing ropes suspended from the ceiling ready to spring in to life just as soon as PE lessons started.

Smiling down on us beatifically from each of the four corners of the hall were life-sized portraits of the four leaders whose names inspired the school house system: Archbishop William Temple, the renowned theologian; Dr David Livingstone, the medical missionary; Sir Wilfred Grenfell, another medical missionary and social reformer; and Lord Shaftesbury, the philanthropist and social reformer. All shared one thing in common: they were acknowledged as shining beacons of leadership and they each had a school house named in their honour. So the four school houses became known as Temple, Livingstone, Shaftesbury and Grenfell. It's only now, reflecting on this more than forty years later, that I realise none of the houses were named after inspirational women, which just goes to show how deeply entrenched sexist attitudes were during the seventies.

Where was Nightingale House, in honour of the esteemed nurse? Or Pankhurst House? Or Fry house, in recognition of Elizabeth Fry, the prisoner reformer and Christian philanthropist? In my seventies schooldays, notions of girl power and the burgeoning women's lib movement were still a world away from the head teacher Mr Peirse and school governors at St Aidan's. The activist Germaine Greer, regarded as one of the architects of women's lib, and her feminist sisters might have been making waves across the globe but barely a ripple reached our sleepy rural backwater.

How gratifying it is to hear that the current school house system celebrates the achievements of notable women! Today's pupils can look up to Florence Nightingale and Helen Keller, the deaf-blind political activist and anti-poverty campaigner, as role models for outstanding citizenship. These two female exemplars sit alongside explorer Sir Edmund Hillary and Charles Babbage, mathematician and engineer, to make up the quartet of school house leaders.

Behind the school hall were the boys' and girls' showers and changing rooms. Outside, to the left of the main hall, was a quad area featuring a small garden planted with shrubs, flanked by the staffroom on one side and a covered walkway on the opposite side. A perimeter path linked the changing rooms to the rear door of the main classroom block. There were two playgrounds, one to the front of the main classroom block and the other to the side, beyond the covered walkway. Steps took you down to the tennis courts (which also, later, doubled up as a playground) and beyond these were expansive playing fields incorporating an athletics track, football and hockey pitches, and a cricket pitch. When we started school, work had also begun on building a brand-new sports pavilion. This was a ground-breaking community participation project involving local businesses, parents, staff and pupils in its construction.

Although the basic structure of St Aidan's hasn't really changed much over the years, its size certainly has. Today, with its plush library and resource centre, IT suites, music and language blocks, lecture theatre and purpose-built sports hall, the school sprawls across several acres.

To my timid eleven-year-old eyes, secondary school was a big and scary place to be. On my first day at school I can remember feeling very small. Before I'd even set my foot inside, I'd feared getting lost in the labyrinth of corridors. It turned into a self-fulfilling prophecy when I feebly knocked on the door of what I thought was my English class.

'Is this first-year class 'A' English?' I timidly asked the tall, bespectacled, ferocious-looking teacher who barked, 'No, this is fourth-year science. Turn left down the corridor, down the stairs and go right to the end.'

Whereas at primary school I'd grown used to being a big fish in a small pond, here the reverse was true. But these fish seemed much more threatening and boisterous than any of those at my primary school; walking along the corridors, you were pushed and jostled by children who seemed so much older and bigger and more worldly wise than you.

As new starters, we also had to get used to a lesson timetable. In Mr Shelley's world there had been no such thing as structured learning; now we had to become acquainted with double maths on a Monday morning, English and French in the afternoon; double English on Tuesday afternoons, followed by domestic science on Wednesdays, or something like that. That, at any rate, was the drift of it. We were streamed according to ability and, for some reason, I was allocated a place in the 'A' stream, the top stream for every subject, though in the case of my maths ability this decision turned out to be questionable, and I was swiftly moved down to the middle group after my end-of-term maths test.

After Mr Shelley's almost non-existent teaching, I found

myself immersed in a whole new world of learning and discovery. It was almost as if we Pilling kids came into secondary education as skeletons needing to be filled out with the blood and muscle of new knowledge, fattened and nourished by learning. And this particular skeleton was in danger of gorging herself.

15

'ABC'

During English classes, I soon became friends with nouns and verbs and adjectives. They were concepts that had been alien to me at primary school, but I found myself developing a feel for language and a love of reading and words. Our form tutor, Mr Maund, also taught us English. Unfortunately, his enthusiasm for his subject could not be matched by his ability to control a class of unruly first formers. It didn't take long for the more boisterous pupils in the class to get the measure of him. They would start making a low humming noise as soon as his back was turned; he would spin round from the blackboard, face flushed, voice spluttering in anger, 'Be-e-e Qu-i-et!' But his charges were too canny for him, and he rarely managed to catch the culprit.

After a term or two of Mr Maund's teaching, we had another English teacher, Miss Borthwick, who was the deputy head teacher, and an entirely different kettle of fish: strict, stern-faced and haughty. Waiting for her in the classroom, we would hear her coming along the corridor, high heels clattering, keys jangling. This was a cue for us to scrape our chairs back and stand up to attention as she swept regally through the door.

As befitted her status, Miss Borthwick demanded respect and recognition of her authority. 'Sit down,' she would proclaim icily, lips pursed before chalking various combinations of conjunctions, verbs, and adverbs on the blackboard in neat handwriting. Though she was aloof, I enjoyed Miss Borthwick's teaching and especially her comprehension and composition sessions.

As far as my primary maths lessons went, I felt I was entering a whole new country. Where Mr Shelley's idea of teaching went little beyond the basic addition and subtraction we needed when playing shop, secondary school found us plunged into an alien world of fractions and percentages, algebra and trigonometry. In my pencil case lurked a set square, protractor and a compass but not, alas, a calculator. These handy devices, taken for granted by today's youngsters, were still a decade or so away. The nearest we had to a calculator was a ready reckoner with tables showing you how to work out some of your calculations. But even that had its limitations; it was far better if you had a dad who could help you to work things out, as I had.

Those classmates who had gone to other primary schools already had a head start on us poor kids from Pilling School. Thanks to our virtually non-existent maths education, we found ourselves behind as we struggled to grasp concepts that were alien to us. Just to make matters worse, I discovered I was woefully lacking in any kind of mathematical aptitude; the teacher might as well have been talking Chinese. Numbers quite literally didn't add up, as far as I was concerned.

Nor did it help that the maths teacher, Mr Ingram, was a strict disciplinarian who used to shout and bawl at his pupils, and wasn't averse to using a slipper to control his unrulier charges. I would quiver in class, hoping Mr Ingram wouldn't ask me a question that would expose my weakness and humiliate me in front of everyone. By some dint of good fortune, he left me alone. Perhaps it's because he remembered me as a child and knew my family, for we were near-neighbours of his when we lived in Elletson Terrace.

There was a huge shock awaiting us when we returned to school after the Whitsuntide holidays in the summer of 1970: the head teacher Mr Peirse summoned us all in to assembly. He had an announcement to make: Mr Ingram had died suddenly during the holidays. He'd suffered a massive heart attack while staying at the home of his daughter. He was just fifty-two years old. Mr Ingram's death stunned the whole community, for not only was he known for his teaching, he was also a local councillor, a previous Mayor and a long-standing member of Preesall Urban District Council. His name lives on through a classroom block for teaching modern languages and health education dedicated in his honour.

A new teacher, Mr Evans, joined the staff as head of mathematics in January 1971, and he became my maths teacher. His arrival must have been a baptism of fire because it was just before 'decimal day' on 15 February 1971, marking the launch of a brand-new standardised system of currency and metric measurement.

Decimal day heralded a radical overhaul of the old pound, shilling and pence method of spending money. Out went the familiar old coins, such as the shilling, threepenny bit, florin (worth two shillings) and half-crown (worth two shillings and sixpence). In came the new ten-pence and five-pence pieces and, eventually, the fifty-pence coin, which replaced the ten-shilling note. This, together with a whole new way of calculating currency that involved using ten as the base, was what decimalisation was all about. It's something we all take for granted today, but back then it was all very new and strange, ushered in on a fanfare of publicity, backed by a massive public education campaign.

None of it was rocket science, even for someone non-mathematical like me, but for months we seemed to hear of little else. In the build up to decimal day, we were bombarded by television programmes and adverts showing how the new system worked. There was even a daft song, 'Decimalisation' by Max Bygraves, recorded on the Pye record label, and I seem to remember my mum was one of hordes of people who went to specially arranged evening classes showing people how to get to grips with this strange new way of calculating the price of a loaf of bread. And yet today we would probably look back and wonder what all the fuss was about.

Mr Evans was pleasant and approachable. But despite him being less threatening than Mr Ingram had been, I wasn't any more comfortable with maths. I can remember going home in tears and my poor dad having to explain to me patiently how to work out a simple fraction. Sometimes even my dad was perplexed by some of the questions we were set in homework and it fell to my new-found friend, Janice Cookson, to help me out. She was a whizz-kid at maths. On many occasions I ended up copying her work on the school bus on the day our homework was due in. However, there were times when even Janice got the answers wrong and I'd managed to copy her wrong answers in my book. Naturally, Mr Evans latched on to this and made some sarcastic comment along the lines of, 'Well, I see you and Janice have managed to get all the same questions wrong. Coincidence or what?'

The relief when I came near to the bottom in my end-of-term maths test and was sent down to the next set, the 'B' group or middle stream, was indescribable.

Our French teacher, Mr Dakin, looked and behaved like the archetypal eccentric professor. He wore small wire-framed spectacles, a white collarless shirt, a shabby beige jacket and tatty brown shoes, minus socks. He indulged in curious acts, such as brushing his teeth in a sink in the corner of his classroom during lessons or muttering to himself as he chalked up French nouns on the blackboard.

On one hot summer's day he took us outside to the playing fields for our lesson. As we sat on the grassy slope, he broke off from his teaching to make a bizarre proposal.

'Look around you,' he ordered, his face deadly serious. 'There are tiny elephants in this grass. Can you see them?' I can remember us all covering our faces with our hands to stifle an explosion of giggles.

Like many academics, his eccentricity masked an impressive intellect; unfortunately for us, though, it did little to enhance our learning. I can recall him passing French textbooks around the classroom and insisting that we read through them. He would then pick pupils out randomly and ask them to read out relevant words and phrases. It was hardly inspiring teaching and it left me completely unenthused by French. Even today, the idea of learning French, or indeed any language, leaves me cold.

Science was delivered as separate lessons in physics, biology and chemistry. I remember feeling intimidated by the science laboratory with its whooshing gas taps, hissing Bunsen burners and 'rotten egg' sulphuric acid smells, fearful that one of my experiments would go awry and cause an explosion. It didn't help that our chemistry teacher was sour-faced Miss Fish, who looked as if she had been pickled in sulphur and did little to make her subject enticing. Biology lessons were memorable for the gruesome dissection experiments we were forced to observe. In one, our biology teacher, Mr Marsh, set about dissecting a mouse in what turned out to be an exercise memorable for its stomach-churning intensity.

History, geography, art, music and French also featured in our timetable. Our geography teacher spent most of his time sitting at his desk reading a newspaper. He would issue us with a textbook and order us to copy out the relevant sections in our class books in neat handwriting. Perhaps he shouldn't have been surprised when, during a geography test, one of his pupils relocated the Falkland Islands to the north of Scotland.

16

'Let's Talk About Sex'

Though English was my favourite subject, I also enjoyed health education. This was taught by Miss Bennett, who was also our PE teacher. She was tiny, with many of her pupils towering over her. But what she lacked in stature she made up for in dynamism and drive. Neatly dressed in kilted skirts and polo T-shirts, her hair was always immaculate. She was a very diligent teacher who schooled us in all the different parts of the anatomy and drilled in to us the importance of good health and hygiene.

Thanks to her I have an encyclopaedic knowledge of the human skeleton, muscles and membrane – or 'memmmbranes' as Miss Bennett used to enunciate, as if to emphasise the importance of these vital bodily functions. I can still confidently name every bone in the human body and describe the function of the pituitary gland in clinical depth. I can't claim this to be a reflection of any academic prowess on my part; it's more a reflection of Miss Bennett's committed teaching and enthusiasm for her subject.

I can remember producing a workbook with bright, technicolour drawings of the human brain and heart in all their vivid glory. Miss Bennett's teaching style was very visual, so any work we produced in our exercise books that was eye-catchingly graphic would be rewarded with higher marks. Miss Bennett also taught human biology as a new GCE O-level subject, and later in her career she broke new ground when she delivered health education as part of a broader PSHE – Personal, Social and Health Education – curriculum. With such a dedicated teacher, it's perhaps not surprising that I, along with several of Miss Bennett's former pupils, went on to develop a career in healthcare, albeit much later in life.

During sex education or 'reproduction' as it was then euphemistically known, the girls were taught separately from the boys, the lads being taught by Mr Gledhill. It was here that Miss Bennett's composure gave way to embarrassed stammering as she described the functions of sperm and ova and explained the act of sexual intercourse and subsequent pregnancy. Because St Aidan's was a church school, Church of England policy decreed that any mention of sex had to be couched in strictly biological terms; this meant that topics such as contraception and dealing with the consequences of unintended pregnancy were definite no-go areas. That said, we were blushingly naïve back then so any discussion of contraception would have caused us as much embarrassment as poor Miss Bennett.

Fast forward forty or more years and sex education is very much a key part of the PSHE curriculum, with worldly wise youngsters armed with an array of knowledge on contraception – and in some schools issued with free condoms, as well. How do I know this? Because for several years I had a job as health promotion specialist for secondary schools and young people, a role which involved working with teachers, school nurses and parents to advise them on sex education. In a society where teenagers today are bombarded with images of sex and sexuality, our approach was seen as a pragmatic solution to a sensitive issue as teenage pregnancy rates spiralled back in the nineties.

Domestic science and needlework were also single-sex lessons. While the girls learnt how to make toast, boil an egg and stitch a hem, the boys were busily engaged in woodwork and metalwork lessons where, among other things, they were taught how to handcraft wooden ashtrays and matchbox holders –

objects which would doubtless have today's anti-smoking lobby throwing up their hands in horror!

Oh yes, the gender stereotypes and expectations were none too subtle: we girls were being groomed for a future role as homemakers while the boys were learning the foundations for a career in one of the masculine trades – joinery, building or lathe work. For, in truth, despite the passing of two decades, expectations for girls of my age hadn't really progressed much from my mother's generation of fifties housewives.

The idea of a boy doing cookery or a girl trying her hand at woodwork was anathema to most young people, and something the school didn't encourage. Those boys brave enough to opt to try their hand at cookery, or girls who fancied working on the lathe (and they tended to be very much in the minority), soon found themselves being teased and taunted mercilessly by their classmates. It was a world removed from today's curriculum where cookery, sewing, metalwork, and woodwork are delivered to both sexes as part of a broader-based design and technology curriculum incorporating a whole range of technical skills, including engineering and graphic design.

Our domestic science teacher was prissy red-haired, Miss Morgan. I can recall our first lesson, for it involved making tea and toast. But this was no ordinary tea and toast; it had to be presented neatly on a tray accompanied by napkins and served to the standards of The Ritz. Miss Morgan came round to inspect our work, sniffing her nose if a napkin wasn't folded correctly; or we'd left crumbs on the tray; or failed to use the strainer when pouring the tea; or failed to apply jam to all four corners of the toast; or, horror of horrors, burnt the toast. There was a certain gentility and finesse to Miss Morgan's brand of teaching that only served to reinforce notions of domestic science as 'feminine' or 'girly.'

This was in the days before TV chefs such as Gordon Ramsay, Jamie Oliver and Paul Hollywood had donned their oven gloves and put a macho spin on the art of cooking. Back then, male chefs such as 'Galloping Gourmet', Graeme Kerr were very much a minority breed. Looking back, they seemed to have about as much panache as a collapsed souffle, lacking the celebrity cachet of Ramsay and co. It was women who were seen as the culinary experts, with the likes of Delia Smith, Mary Berry and Marguerite Patten seen as self-appointed queens of the kitchen.

One of the earliest TV chefs was Fanny Cradock, a frightful-looking woman whose outrageous make-up, distinctive arched eyebrows and formidable, snooty manner gave her an appearance akin to a pantomime dame. Fanny's husband, Major Johnnie would hover timidly in the background as her henpecked assistant.

In my first year at St Aidan's I learnt how to make crispy scones, sausage plait and quiche Lorraine, which I would proudly carry home in my wicker basket to present to my family who would eagerly devour them. Naturally, as I had already been taught baking skills by my granny, I felt that in domestic science, if nothing else, I had a head start on many of my classmates.

School dinners back then were similar to those dished up at primary school. They usually consisted of traditional fare such as hotpot, beef stew, toad-in-the-hole and boiled fish, served up with the inevitable salty mashed potatoes and limp, boiled cabbage. This would be followed by a stodgy pudding of some kind – jam roly-poly, Bakewell tart with lashings of custard, rice pudding – washed down with water (no cans of pop then). As school food went, it was good, nourishing, no-frills fare. But we were a world away from the consumer-driven canteen-style food service with its array of hot and cold dishes, including nutritious salads, imaginative quiches and pasta dishes, created to tempt the palates of students today.

One of the bugbears about school dinners was being forced to queue in the corridor for meals. There was a pecking order of service that correlated with age; as humble first-years we were inevitably among the last to sit down, by which time our gravy and potatoes had congealed to a lukewarm mush. It was the older pupils, usually prefects, who controlled the lunch queues, behaving like miniature officers of the Gestapo if any of us stepped out of line.

By the end of my second year of interminable lunch queues, I'd grown tired of queuing up for food that was pallid and unappealing by the time it reached my mouth. I persuaded my mum to let me take a packed lunch to school. My Tupperware lunch box was crammed with ham or chicken paste sandwiches and a packet of crisps. All my friends were doing the same, and it seemed almost trendy to be seen taking your own lunch to school. Healthy eating it wasn't, and it perhaps explains why I was starving and intent on raiding the biscuit tin for custard creams by the time I got home from school. Although I wasn't overweight, my pudgy arms, double chin and thickening waist were testimony to a diet that could hardly be described as wholesome.

17

'It's All in the Game'

If I felt at home in domestic science, PE was an area where I knew I was woefully lacking in confidence or ability. During netball I felt awkward and ungainly, a veritable clumsy elephant. It was a legacy I carried from Mr Shelley, who never lost an opportunity to remind me how clumsy I was. Try as I might, I couldn't manage either to defend or attack; it didn't matter which position I was assigned to – wing attack, goal defence, goal attack – I felt useless, my raised arms flailing hopelessly in the air as I tried to grab a ball that always seemed to elude me. I could only marvel at the nimble, panther-like moves of my teammates, at their hunger, speed and accuracy.

Things got so bad that I can remember nearly knocking the lights out of the opposite team's star attacker, a sporty girl called Karen Johnson, as she launched herself up to score. As I leapt up to knock the ball out of the way, I ended up punching her in the face instead. The game had to be halted while Miss Bennett attended to the poor girl, who was sporting the beginning of a dubious-looking black eye, her face creased with tears of pain and humiliation. Back then, the sporty girls were nearly always shiny-faced and supercharged with confidence, popular with their peers and teachers alike. This had another knock-on effect on my already fragile self-esteem, eroded by years of Mr Shelley's cruel regime; I equated sporting success with social recognition and acceptance, and I felt I'd failed dismally at both.

My lack of sporting prowess was brought home to me even more painfully when I suffered the ignominy of not being picked to represent my house, Temple house, in the first-year netball contest. During sports events, Temple pupils had the honour of wearing a navy blue bib, reflecting the house colours. Alas, I never got to wear one because I was never good enough to be selected for the netball team. There were perhaps a dozen or more of us first-year girls in Temple house, and I can still vividly remember wincing as the names of the netball team were read out, fearful that mine would not be among them. Sure enough, my fears were confirmed when the Temple netball captain, Elaine Norris, older sister of that shy blond-haired boy in my class, called out the last names.

'Oh, please, just let me be anything, even if it's just a substitute,' I pray inwardly – but to no avail. I look around me. All of the first-year Temple girls have been selected to represent the house team, bar me and one other. It means that she and I are consigned to spending that lesson reading a book in the library. I feel like a swot – and a failure.

Hockey, I seemed to fare a little better at. I enjoyed the rough and tumble of hockey and given time I might have made a half-decent player but, alas, it wasn't a game that we played often enough for me to master any skills; netball was always favoured over hockey as the activity of choice, perhaps because the hockey pitch always seemed to be waterlogged. Nor did I shine in tennis, athletics or badminton; though one year, I was chosen as part of the Temple house relay team during sports day and can remember trembling with trepidation at the mere thought of dropping the baton or mistiming my handover.

Given my abysmal sporting record, it's perhaps not surprising that in my end-of-year school report Miss Bennett always graded me as C-plus, with the comment, 'Angela tries hard in her endeavours.' To my mind, that's a euphemism for, 'she's rubbish really' although Miss Bennett, to be fair, wouldn't quite have put it that way.

It's funny because some time after leaving school I managed to reinvent myself as something of a fitness fanatic, taking up non-competitive activities such as aerobics after it was popularised by the likes of Jane Fonda in the eighties. During my late forties, I discovered the joys of running. I've completed half-marathons, albeit at a slow pace, and have set my sights on a full marathon. Perhaps all the time, beneath that shy, gauche teenager of all those years ago, there was a sporty girl trying to break out.

One of the things I hated about PE was the compulsory showers after games. And I know I was far from alone in this. There was always a collective groan when we had to go in to the communal showers because it meant our naked bodies being fully exposed, without as much as a curtain to protect our modesty. We were pubescent eleven-year-olds, going on twelve, encountering different stages of bodily development. Some of us had already sprouted breasts, others hadn't. Some of us were chubby, others were stick thin.

But whatever our shape, none of us liked having our blossoming womanhood scrutinised. Having a period was always a good way of getting out of games, and out of the flesh-crawling embarrassment of those dreaded showers. You'd get your mother to write a note excusing you from games on the basis of your 'monthly.' Or you'd write that note yourself, somehow managing to forge your mum's signature, the oldest trick in the book. And it's funny, really, how so many of us in those days seemed to have irregular frequent periods that might have warranted a visit to a gynaecologist …

I think somewhere along the line someone got the message, for I seem to remember after my first or second year at school, open communal showers were phased out. PE staff finally understood that communal showering was just too embarrassing for young girls on the threshold of adolescence. But in the end it was a pragmatic decision which drew this practice to a halt: as school numbers grew and classroom space became tighter, the showers and changing rooms were converted to temporary classrooms.

It was about this time that I managed to persuade my mum to buy me my first bra, a dainty pink-and-white gingham affair from British Home Stores. Having a bra was a sort of status symbol, a sure sign that you were dancing towards womanhood.

18

Take Your Partners...

If the wet weather put paid to outdoor PE, there was little cause for celebration. An announcement that games were 'off' was invariably greeted with collective muttering and mumbling, for it meant one thing: country dancing. We would have to make our way to the school hall for an hour or so of dancing, or nearly two hours if it happened to be a double games lesson, as it usually was. Dance classes meant watching Mr Gledhill and Miss Bennett demonstrate the moves for the barn dance, American square dancing, and German clap dancing. Each routine involved a complicated sequence of jigs and reels, twists and turns, to accompanying accordion music.

In an attempt to recreate the etiquette of the fifties dance hall, Mr Gledhill ordered us to sit in rows on opposite sides of the hall, boys one side and the girls on the other. The lads had to walk across the floor, select a dance partner and politely invite their chosen lassie to dance. This might have been fine if we'd been older, more self-assured young people, sun-ripened for romantic pickings. But we were barely out of primary school, ungainly and much too young to appreciate the charms of the opposite sex. It led to a lot of embarrassment, giggling and smirking on both sides of the room; the cheeky spotty-faced boys were clearly far more at home kicking a football around in the playground than requesting girl's hand for a dance. And as for we girls, well, we simply hated the sight of these snotty-nosed young wretches, a feeling that was almost certainly reciprocated.

It made for some pretty awkward couplings. For some reason, I seemed to attract Stuart Bailey, the earnest school swot, as my regular dance partner. He would shuffle across the room, stiff-legged, face beetroot-red, eyes averted to the floor as he blushingly asked me if I would care to dance, with about as much conviction as if he'd invited me to share an arsenic-flavoured lolly. Still, he was destined for bigger and better things, for he later went on to take a convincing role as the dame in the school pantomime. I never did find out what happened to him after he left school, though I suspect he may have found a niche in life in amateur dramatics.

Once we'd been paired up with our respective partners, it was our turn to dance. I think we could have justifiably renamed our version of *Strictly Come Dancing* as 'Strictly Rum(bustious) Dancing!' In one routine, which I seem to remember was known as 'stripping the willow' we were required to form two lines, boys in one line and girls aligned opposite their partners. The couple at the end had to link arms and skip down the middle of the two rows, breaking off at the end. Each partner would then skip round the back of their lines, and the rest of their row would follow. The whole routine would start again with the next couple taking the lead. That, at least, is the gist of the dance as far as my hazy recollections will allow, though I may have missed some of the finer technical details.

Picture forty or more reluctant, awkward, ungainly twelve-year-olds, and you might imagine the scene of chaos that ensued. Some of the lads ended up going faster than the music called for and we ended up tripping and falling over each other, dancing with about as much finesse and conviction as a herd of young bullocks.

But if I hated country dancing, there was another activity that I really enjoyed, and that was contemporary dance. Miss Bennett headed modern dance classes; these appealed

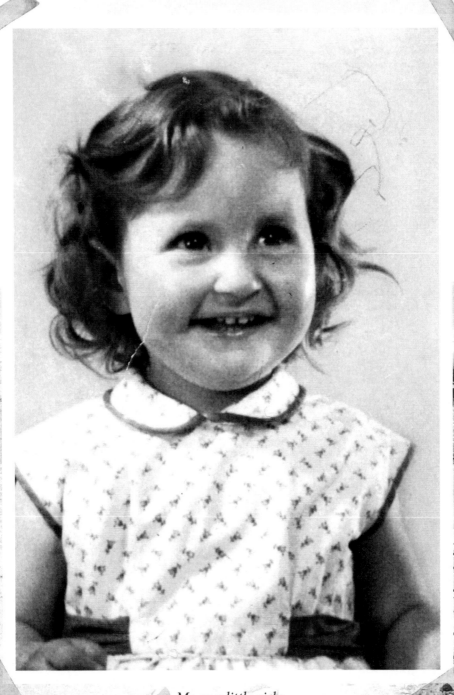

Me as a little girl.

With classmates at Fleetwood Charity School.
I am third from the left on the front row.

Pilling Youth Club
I am in the front row, far right
Photo by Graham Curwen.

In Mr Maund's form at St Aidan's.
I am on the second row from the front, seated, third from the right.
Photo by Scholastic Souvenirs, Blackpool.

Mum, me and my brother Geoff at Manchester Airport.

Mum and Dad's Wedding day.
With left, Granny and Grandad and right,
Grandma and Grandad Bill.

Grandma Allen.

*Keith and me on our wedding day at
the ludicrously young age of 21.*

Me as a junior reporter at the Garstang Courier

to youngsters like me who were not suited to competitive sports such as netball. I found myself in my element, moving expressively to the theme music from the western, *The Good, the Bad and the Ugly,* trying to capture the mood of the music, unleashing a hitherto unknown creative side as I shimmied and swayed to the haunting melodies.

During modern dance lessons, the clumsiness and awkwardness I'd felt when taking part in traditional sports was banished, along with my inhibitions.

St Aidan's was ahead of its time as far as the arts went; every year the school organised a popular inter-house arts contest, with competitions in dance, music, needlework and cookery. I can recall representing Temple house, dancing to a catchy instrumental tune, 'Cast Your Fate to the Wind' by sixties jazz-inspired group Sounds Orchestral.

The school was also renowned for its pantomime tradition. The Christmas pantomime, written by the head teacher Mr Peirse and performed by pupils from across the school, was a glitzy extravaganza worthy of the West End. It was the undisputed highlight of the school year, attracting sell-out audiences. I can remember my time in the spotlight as a chorus girl in *Cinderella*. We had to audition for the part, which meant singing a few bars of a tune (I can't remember which one) to Miss Borthwick's piano accompaniment. Those who know me will testify that I cannot sing tunefully but I must have sounded the right notes because I was thrilled to hear I'd been offered a place in the chorus.

The part of Cinderella was played beautifully by Karen Slater, a pretty blonde girl, with Susan Butler as her Prince Charming. But it was Stuart Bailey, my country dance partner, who brought the house down with his convincingly camp Baron Hardup. We all-singing, all-dancing chorus girls wore full polka-dot skirts in turquoise and blue, teamed with turquoise boleros. We danced to country-style routines choreographed by Miss Bennett, with all the aplomb of seasoned pros. One of our songs was 'Getting to Know You,' from the *The King and I* and another was Irving Berlin's 'You're Just in Love (I Wonder Why).' Taking part in the pantomime was great fun for all of us, and I can still remember the palpable buzz of being a tiny part of such a big production.

My second pantomime, *Aladdin*, came in 1972, when I was in my fourth year at St Aidan's. This time I was given was a backstage role, as prompt. I can remember sitting perched on a chair in the wings, feeling very important as I scoured the pages of script methodically to make sure I could interject with a timely prompt in the event of an actor fluffing his or her lines. My friend Janice Cookson took the lead part of Aladdin, but it was Stuart Bailey who brought the house down as Widow Twankey.

During one rehearsal, Mr Peirse chastised me for not being quick enough off the mark when one of the leading players stuttered. After his telling off, I made doubly sure I was word-ready during the performances. For some unfathomable reason, I can also remember Keith Norris, that shy boy from Pilling, having a backstage role as props assistant.

One of the best things about *Aladdin* was that the pantomime took priority over schoolwork. It meant we got out of lessons because of all the hours of rehearsals we had to attend. Like seasoned pros, we were even treated to an afternoon off school prior to one of the performances. This was because Mr Peirse was concerned that we would be tired and jaded if we had to deliver a show after a full day of lessons. I can remember us all being trudged along by our teachers on a nature walk across the windswept lanes of Arm Hill towards the shore, instructed by Mr Peirse to enjoy some fresh air and a break from all the frenzy of pantomime. It was cold and windy but it was infinitely better than doing double maths.

Being part of a pantomime production team was great for boosting confidence and self-esteem and it became a springboard for many shy St Aidan's youngsters, propelling them into careers in dance and drama. Alas, I was never destined for the bigger stage, preferring life out of the spotlight – unless it was under the disco spotlight, more of which later.

19

'Rebel Rebel'

Our head teacher, Mr Peirse, was a stout, bespectacled, bulbous-nosed, plain-talking disciplinarian who hailed from Northumbria and walked with the gait of a farmer. He ruled with a rod of iron and was uncompromising in his standards. Yet he managed to command the respect of staff, parents and pupils alike. With Mr Peirse it was a case of what you saw was what you got, and people liked that quality in him. He was firm but fair, and was recognised as much a leader at Wyre Magistrates' Court, where he chaired the Juvenile Bench, as he was in school. But step out of line with Mr Peirse and you knew the consequences. Perhaps, in truth, we were scared stiff of him, though he was very different from Mr Shelley: underneath his authoritarian sternness was a man of humanity, driven by a desire to see all of his pupils do their best; he was a benevolent dictator. He prided himself on knowing the names of all of his charges and tried to instil in each of us a sense of pride and purpose in school.

He had his pet hates, and one of these was smoking (pilfering and showing dissent to his authority were among the others). Any pupil caught having a crafty puff outside school, on the school bus, or in school grounds risked his wrath. Punishment was The Cane and it wasn't done quietly. When Mr Peirse used The Cane, it was intended as a stern warning for the rest of us as to what would happen if we were caught in possession of the dreaded weed, not to mention a lesson in public humiliation for the unfortunate young perpetrator.

On the day of the caning, the whole school would be ordered to file into the assembly hall. Mr Peirse would march down the centre of the hall, shoes clacking, face crimson, puffed out with purpose, wielding his cane. We all waited with anxious breaths, as the culprit – or culprits, because often there was more than one – awaited their fate. In his booming voice, Mr Peirse would deliver a sombre lecture on the perils of smoking, before marching the shame-faced young offenders out of the hall to his office down the corridor, where they would be thwacked across the knuckles with a brisk, clean stroke, leaving them smarting with pain and humiliation. It was a salutary lesson for all of us: smoking doesn't just kill, it doesn't do your street cred much good either. Such was the climate of fear induced by The Cane, I can remember some pupils actually ended up fainting.

It would never have occurred to us, or our parents, to question Mr Peirse's use of The Cane. Corporal punishment, consisting of a thwack of The Cane, or being whacked across the head by the slipper, or having a blackboard duster thrust in your direction, was generally accepted as a method of controlling unruly pupils, just in the same way our parents wouldn't think twice about administering a short, sharp smack across the legs or buttocks. It seems strange to think of this, in these days of child protection and safeguarding.

Mr Peirse's aversion to cigarettes was ironic given that, if you had occasion to knock on the school staffroom door at any time, the chances were you wouldn't be able to see from one end of the room to the other thanks to the fog of thick, choking cigarette smoke, not to mention the quick surreptitious hiding of offending fags by teachers caught red-handed by one of their pupils.

In case I convey the impression that The Cane was a regular ritual at St Aidan's, it's worth saying that canings were, in reality, rare events. And it's precisely because of this that they carried the shock factor. It's a bit like watching horror films, really. Watch too many and you risk becoming desensitised. In the same way, had we observed too many canings we would, I'm sure, have become inured to their effects. As it was, The Cane became an effective deterrent for any of us tempted by the idea of taking up tobacco. The consequences, in terms of having the whole school know your pain and humiliation, were just too awful to contemplate.

Now, of course, smoking among young people is sadly commonplace, even among primary-aged children. When, years later, I worked as a health promotion specialist supporting primary schools to develop no-smoking policies, I was horrified to learn that children as young as eight were addicted to nicotine, with many becoming habitual smokers by the time they reached secondary school. No doubt Mr Peirse would turn in his grave in horror over the high prevalence of smoking – not to mention weed, Es, speed, coke, meow meow, special K and the host of other mind-blowing legal and illegal substances common among today's young people but virtually unknown or unheard of among my own sheltered generation of rural kids.

At St Aidan's there was another, more wholesome, reason for the whole school to congregate: the daily assembly was considered an important part of the fabric of school life. Every morning everyone, staff and pupils, would be ordered into the hall for the fifteen-minute service. This routine changed on Fridays, when assembly was held in the afternoon to mark the end of the school week. With fewer than two hundred pupils in the entire school, it was relatively easy to fit everyone inside the hall.

School assembly was considered to be a vital opener to the school day, providing pupils and staff with a kind of moral and spiritual porridge to get the day off to a good start, and to sustain and nourish. Assembly was ordered and planned with military precision. Each form was ordered to file into the hall, one form at a time, with places arranged in order of seniority. The first and second-year pupils were required to sit cross-legged near the front of the stage, and there'd always be much shuffling and fidgeting going on. Older pupils were allocated seats in order of seniority, with the fifth-years sitting near the back of the hall, supposedly on account of their growing maturity.

During assembly we had to wear our plimsolls, which made a squeaky noise as they rubbed against the surface of the maplewood varnished floor, the unmistakable pong of sweaty feet competing with the waxy whiff of industrial floor polish. Shoes were prohibited because of the risk of damage to the floor. Exceptions to this rule were Mr Peirse and his deputy, Miss Borthwick. Mr Peirse would make his grand entrance, striding down the school hall purposefully, shoes clacking, while the assembled pupils stood to attention in respectful silence as he climbed the steps to the rostrum with all the aplomb of a king or a senior politician. Miss Borthwick wore high heels that clickety-clacked down the aisle.

On stage, Mr Peirse was flanked by Miss Borthwick, some senior teachers, the head boy and girl and a group of bored-looking fifth-year prefects, hand-picked for their leadership qualities.

'Good morning, boys and girls,' Mr Peirse would announce sonorously, as he glanced over the lectern at his young charges and prepared to impart his words of wisdom to the snuffling assembled pupils.

Assembly usually consisted of school notices; the reading of a lesson from the *Bible* by a pupil or teacher, or visiting clergyman; prayers; a couple of hymns; and a short address from Mr Peirse imparting a Christian or moral message. Hymns were sung to the accompaniment of music teacher Miss Cauldwell's piano playing. Miss Cauldwell was a fine musician, but she had a habit of hitting her notes at a gallop so that as we sung 'Onward

Christian Soldiers' or 'Love Divine, All Love's Excelling' we found ourselves vocally sprinting to keep up with her. It meant that each hymn was sung at breakneck speed, and we'd reach the last verse before you could so much as utter the word 'Jerusalem.'

Aside from assembly and canings, I can remember another occasion when the whole school had to congregate in the hall. It was to watch the investiture of The Prince of Wales at Caernarfon Castle, on 1 July 1969. The ceremony was screened on a large-screen television which had been set up on the school stage. I can remember being bored to tears by the long speeches, some of them in Welsh. But then, it did have its compensations because it meant we got out of lessons for the afternoon.

20

'When Irish Eyes are Smiling'

Each year, the maths teacher, Mr Ingram, organised a school holiday to Ireland. During my first year at St Aidan's, I managed to persuade my parents to let me go away on my first holiday without them. I was probably one of the youngest in a party of twenty-five or so pupils and two or three members of staff, including the girls' PE teacher, Miss Bennett. We sailed from Liverpool to Dublin, staying in a guest house in Bray, just outside Dublin. Bray was, and still is, a popular seaside town, along with its near-neighbour, Greystones. We stayed at a guest house, and I shared a room with three or four older girls.

Mr Ingram was much more relaxed on holiday than he was in the classroom. There were times when he could be quite funny, cracking jokes and teasing us. I recall him being accompanied on holiday by one of his friends, a character called Artie Smith, who came to Preesall from County Roscommon to work for ICI. There was always plenty of banter between Mr Ingram and Artie.

One of the highlights of our holiday was a tour of the Guinness factory in Dublin. After watching each stage of the brewing process, we were each treated to a small sample glass of the potent velvety brew. It was my first taste of alcohol.

'Now, go easy on this and don't drink it all if you don't like the taste,' counselled Mr Ingram.

'Ugh,' I remember saying as I chocked back the thick, claggy liquid and revolted at its disgusting aftertaste. Yet my street cred prevented me from giving up at the first hurdle; I continued drinking until the last drop had been drained. Over the coming years my relationship with alcohol mellowed, but that first taste of Guinness left me feeling sick.

Later, we visited Dublin city centre, popping in to Clerys, the city's old-fashioned department store, and its more opulent counterpart Switzer's, as we walked down Grafton Street. It all felt very exciting and grown-up to be crossing the main roads in such a busy city, with no parents ordering you to 'mind how you go.'

We toured little country towns by coach, travelling on quiet country roads, and also took a rail journey to Limerick, speeding through lush green pastures. Even then, at the age of twelve, I wasn't too young to appreciate the quaint charm and beauty of the Irish countryside and a way of life that has long-since disappeared.

Back at our guest house in Bray, we spent our free evenings walking up Bray Head, rising to give lovely views across the bay, where on a really clear day you could see as far as Snowdon. But it wasn't the scenery we were interested in; it was the local boys who befriended us and offered to be our guides and chaperones who caught our eyes. So off we would climb up Bray Head, escorted by these boys, always mindful of Miss Bennett's caution to stay together in groups. We were bowled over by their Irish charm and blarney.

Bray also had a fairground and amusement arcade. One night, when visiting the amusement arcade, we encountered an expensively dressed, heavily fringed baby-faced young boy surrounded by an entourage of minders. He was playing on one of the slot machines, and he looked familiar to us. It was none other than child actor Jack Wild, at that time enjoying his brief flash of fame as the Artful Dodger in the film *Oliver*. He was probably the same age as us, yet 'film star' was etched on his face and in his clothing. With feigned indifference, we refrained from asking him for his autograph, preferring to watch his every move covertly from behind the slot machines.

With no mobile phones back then, the cost of making a telephone call home from a public telephone kiosk would have been ruinously expensive. So we were encouraged to write letters to our families letting them know how we were going on, as well as receiving mail from home. I still have copies of the letters my parents and family wrote to me. They give a fascinating insight into the history of the era.

In one, my 'Granny' Pilling, my dad's grandmother who lived in the wooden bungalow adjoining our house with her daughter, Freda, my dad's aunt, wrote:

> *Dear Angela,*
>
> *We hope you are having a nice time and the weather is fine. Everything is going on all right here. I think Geoffrey misses you a bit. They will be going down to the sports day this afternoon. He wanted a pot egg for the races {egg-and-spoon race}... I have been washing today and Freda is picking blackcurrants. I expect you are having some nice outings. You will have lots to tell us... How was it sailing? We hope it wasn't rough.*
>
> *We have been watching the men landing on the moon. It was on television at seven o'clock this morning, but your dad stayed up {all night} to watch it and he promised to wake Geoffrey up to see it, which he did, and it suited Geoffrey, he was so interested in it.*

On the evening of the moon landings, Mr Ingram suggested that we might want to stay up to see world history being made. We watched this momentous event – as Neil Armstrong and Buzz Aldrin took their famed leap forward to become the first men to land on the moon – unfold on a black-and-white television in the lounge of a jaded but homely Irish guest house on 20 July 1969.

The next day, and for weeks afterwards, the TV, radio, and national newspapers were buzzing with news of the moon landings. But I, along with my friends, had more pressing concerns to deal with. Leaving Ireland would mean saying goodbye to those twinkly eyed Irish boys we'd befriended. I can remember tears welling in my eyes as I bade them an emotional farewell before boarding the coach to Dublin for our sail home. Hearing Armstrong proclaim the immortal words, 'This is one giant leap for mankind …' failed to make an impression on me. I was twelve years old, and making my own giant leap into adolescence and all that it entailed.

21

'I Get By with a Little Help from My Friends'

'I get by with a little help from my friends' trilled the Beatles and, later, Joe Cocker. And with a little help from my friends, I managed to survive my tumultuous teenage years. Some of the time it was, yes, even enjoyable and fun! I think of our shared adolescence as a fairground ride of thrills and spills: one minute we'd be soaring high on a roller coaster of dizzying new experiences – dances, youth club and fashion – and the next we'd be bumping along in the dodgem cars crashing into barriers imposed by parent and teachers, not to mention own our self-imposed barriers, spilling out of teen tantrums, from which a refusal to behave in any reasonable kind of way could lead to some pretty spectacular rows.

'No, I'm not wearing that thing!' I'd snarl in response to my mother's gentle insistence that I wear a navy pinafore dress for an outing to my Auntie Peggy's, stomping upstairs to my room. And then in the ensuing row that inevitably followed when I eventually surfaced, showing not the slightest bit of remorse, I would be 'grounded' for my 'obstreperous' behaviour. This shouldn't have come as any surprise to me because it was a scenario that was repeated almost daily. And yet surprise me it did, because I could never see any wrongdoing.

With friends around, you had someone to share your

troubles with. Oh yes, we were drama queens, plumped up with hormones, full of self-pitying woe. But one of the joys of having someone who was going through exactly the same as you, and perhaps even worse if their stories were to be believed, meant you had access to your own exclusive teenage self-help group, where others could chip in with sage advice cultivated from the wisdom of their own parental run-ins.

For the first twelve months at St Aidan's I sought the cushioning and familiarity of my friends from Pilling School. I was delighted that I could resurrect my friendship with my best friend from primary school, Anne Rossall. Having left primary school the year before me, Anne was now a second-year pupil, and during break times I gravitated towards her. But by now she had made her own set of friends and, no doubt, regarded me as a nuisance for wanting to tag along with her.

Among Anne's friendship circle were her half-cousins, Lynn and Anne Bleasdale, Sheila Murro, and another girl from Pilling, Gill Raby. There is one particular memory of this group that stands out for me, and that was when we went on a sponsored walk to raise money towards the building of a new swimming pool in Preesall.

Back then, the Over Wyre district didn't have a pool. A committee was formed to look at ways of raising money to build a facility that could be used by the whole community. One of the ideas that came from this was to organise an eighteen-mile sponsored walk through each of the Wyre villages – Preesall, Knott End, Pilling, Out Rawcliffe, Hambleton, and Stalmine.

I can remember us all signing up for this gruelling route, which started and finished at St Aidan's. By the time we'd reached the Union Moss Road, at Out Rawcliffe – probably just over halfway in to the journey – we were feeling tired and jaded, revived only when someone had the bright idea of switching on their transistor radio and the foot-tapping sounds of Edwin Starr's '25 Miles' came blasting through the airwaves, sending us merrily on our way. An appropriate choice of song in the circumstances.

I don't remember how much money I raised in sponsorship, but I do recall hobbling up the steps of St Aidan's School, close on eight hours after setting off, feet covered in blisters, vowing never to walk that distance again. I suppose, for a twelve-year-old, it was no mean feat. Within what seemed like no time at all, a shiny new pool had risen up from a patch of land within winking distance of St Aidan's, its purpose to teach swimming and life-saving skills to the next generation of Over Wyre school children, as well as becoming a leisure venue for the local community.

Soon after, swimming lessons were introduced as part of our PE curriculum. We had our lessons on a Tuesday afternoon. I can remember the nauseating chlorine smell and the suffocating airless atmosphere in the changing rooms that felt like having a warm, damp towel thrust in front of your face. Perhaps not surprisingly, given my miserable record in PE and sport, I didn't take to swimming like a duck to water – more like a badger to bright sunlight, as I clung desperately to the polystyrene floats that were supposed to keep us buoyant, ignoring the swimming teacher's demands to 'move away from the rail.'

Alas, the swimming pool wasn't destined to live until a ripe old age. Some thirty years or so after its bright and triumphant opening the pool closed in 2007, its demise due to the council decreeing it could neither afford nor justify the costs needed to bring it splashing into the twenty-first century. Clearly they did not have the same sentimental attachment to the pool as did the good folk of Over Wyre, and its loss is mourned by people within the community to this day. Naturally, that includes people like me and my friends who walked our gangly, adolescent legs off to buy those precious bricks.

Over time, I weaned myself away from Anne Rossall's friendship group and started to spend more time among my own peers. I became best friends with Janice Cookson, whose maths homework I'd copied when I first started school. Then there was Lynn Henderson, a cheeky, bubbly twinkly eyed farmer's, daughter; Vivien Cornall who, with her long blonde hair and baby-blue eyes, found herself surrounded by a string of male admirers as she grew older; and straight-talking, comical Enid Cross. They all came from the nearby village of Stalmine.

Janice and I shared a passion for football. But music, fashion, dance and boys were what bound us all – Lynn, Vivien, Enid, Janice and I – back in those halcyon days. We stayed together as friends throughout the five years of secondary school, though there were sometimes moments of high drama when we squabbled or fell out spectacularly.

Typically, it would be over something innocuous that someone had said – a comment about someone's hair, or their dress, or someone feeling excluded from a conversation – and the fallout would be enough to start a third world war, sending one or the other of us in to apoplectic grief. The next day it would be forgotten, and all was candyfloss, sweetness and light again, though sometimes the pain was prolonged, lingering for a few days. I suppose that's the mercurial nature of teenage friendship, and it's probably no different today than it was then, though mercifully we didn't have the added complexities of Facebook, Twitter and selfies to deal with.

22

'I'm a Believer'

Back then, going to church was an important part of the tapestry of rural life. It fulfilled a vital social as well as spiritual function. Concerts, film shows, coffee mornings, garden parties and whist drives were nearly always in some way or other connected to the local church. The church was very much the hub of the community, a role it still has today, though arguably this has been diluted by changing attitudes towards religion.

Most kids went to Sunday school and were later confirmed, and I was no exception. Confirmation was, and still is, an important rite of passage, denoting your status as a fully confirmed member of the Church of England, committed to the faith. It's a tradition that normally takes place at the age of eleven or twelve, though some people who may have missed being confirmed during adolescence choose to have their confirmation in adulthood.

Confirmation was the culmination of many weeks of careful preparation. It meant we Pilling teenagers had to forfeit a chunk of our Saturdays to attend confirmation classes at the imposing vicarage. These were led by the vicar, the Rev. Thomas William Baverstock, a serious looking ex-army chaplain with distinctive long grey, whiskery sideburns, whom you could easily imagine barking his orders to the military. By dint of coincidence, that shy blond boy who had started primary school at the same time as me and was in the same class at secondary school, was also there. However, Keith Norris and I didn't really have much to say to each other.

During classes in Mr Baverstock's magnificent oak-panelled study, we were instructed on the catechism, the Ten Commandments and the Lord's Prayer, and required to recite each of these off by heart. Mrs Baverstock, his perky wife, her iron-grey hair swept in to a neat little bun, would hover in the background, popping into the room with a welcome tray of orange juice and rich tea biscuits halfway through the session.

To our twelve-year-old selves, with more interesting things to occupy us such as kicking a football or riding a bike, it all seemed dull and tedious. But the actual confirmation service was more interesting, for two reasons: firstly because of the flouting of the 'no Brylcreem' rule, and secondly because it gave us girls the chance to dress up.

Prior to the confirmation service – in which we would duly be confirmed as members of the church by the Bishop of Lancaster – Mr Baverstock had carefully issued us with instructions on what to wear and how to receive the bishop's blessing. Boys were told to refrain from wearing Brylcreem. This was because the bishop would be placing his hands on each candidate's head in blessing, and it would be unpleasant for him if his palms were to become smeared in oily hair cream. Not only that, but all the other unfortunate 'confirmees' would risk having their heads anointed with an unctuous lick of Brylcreem as the bishop unwittingly passed his greasy hands over their waiting heads.

On the day of the ceremony, all the boys duly took note of the request not to wear Brylcreem; all, that is, except one: Bill Rooney, a good-looking lad with dark, swarthy features and a mop of thick lustrous black hair. He'd slathered his hair with the stuff, using enough grease and oil to fry a pan of chips. With minutes to go before the start of the service, it was too late to order him home for a hair wash. The rituals proceeded and the bishop put out his hands to bless Bill Rooney's far-from-saintly head with barely a flinch. No doubt he'd seen it all before.

The service, at St James' Church, Stalmine, was a special occasion watched by an entourage of parents, grandparents, godparents and various other family members. Traditionally, girls were expected to dress in bridal white, complete with a veil. I wore a dainty white Crimplene suit with a pleated skirt and matching cardigan, and a white veil. White lacy tights completed the ensemble. The boys dressed smartly in suits, shirt and tie. It was probably the first time in my life I'd had chance to get dressed up. I felt quite grown-up and important.

Today's dress code for confirmation ceremonies seems less formal. Indeed, when our youngest son, Darren, was confirmed in 1994 he threw a wobbly over being ordered to wear a shirt and tie and his best trousers.

'If he wants to wear jeans and they make him feel comfortable, then let him wear jeans – it's no problem,' said the understanding wife of our lovely vicar of the time, the Rev. Terry Middleditch. There would have been no such concessions in our day.

23

'Football Crazy'

After meeting those Irish boys on holiday in Bray, the lads I went to school with seemed dull by comparison. As far as my friends and I were concerned, the boys we shared classroom space with were cheeky, spotty, cocky little wretches, lacking any kind of maturity. Hormonally, we girls were streets ahead of them, having already started to blossom in to puberty. But it didn't mean we were emotionally mature, and the slightest stinging criticism or wrong word to reach our hypersensitive ears would be enough to trigger a torrent of tears.

'You're ugly, you are, France,' I can remember one little weasel-faced lad from Hambleton snarling at me. Today, the older me would have retorted, 'You aren't so pretty yourself.' But the twelve-year-old I inhabited was utterly crushed, devastated by this hammer blow to an already fragile self-esteem, still reeling from Mr Shelley and eleven-plus failure.

I don't think it was a conscious decision, but somehow and somewhere along the line I decided that one way of gaining the respect of boys – and, in some perverse kind of logic, earning some self-respect for myself – was to behave as they did. And so I cultivated a love of football. I wasn't alone in this. Many of my friends, including Gill Raby and Janice Cookson, shared this passion.

Football was a national obsession, very much as it is today; perhaps more so. We didn't have the distractions of Facebook, or

Twitter, or computer consoles. Aligning yourself with a football team was an important feature of your identity. You pinned to your mast the colours of your favourite team and pledged your undying loyalty to them, ready, as advised by Kipling, 'to meet triumph with disaster and treat those two imposters just the same.'

Unlike today's smart-arse players, who seem to think the world owes them their mind-boggling wage packets, footballers in the seventies – even those high on the Richter scale of superstardom – seemed to be aware of their obligation to their fans to play to the best level they could. And they didn't disappoint. It was the era of George Best and his dazzling artistry on the pitch, Bobby Charlton, Rodney Marsh, Billy Bremner, Charlie George and countless others – footballing legends who brought their own brand of magic to the game and entranced and enthralled their legions of fans.

Back then, I was a Manchester United fan, lured by the glamour of Bestie and his footballing comrades Bobby Charlton, Brian Kidd, Willie Morgan, Nobby Stiles, Alex Stepney, and numerous others whose names I would have been able to recount with the speed of lightning. Not only did I know the names of all the Manchester United team, I was pretty familiar with the Leeds United, Liverpool and Chelsea line-ups. And I could boast an encyclopaedic knowledge of every football ground in the country, and name every manager in the Football League with about as much ease as Bestie in one of his famed dribbles.

My knowledge and insight were the result of hours of poring over football books and magazines such as *Shoot!* and Saturday nights glued to *Match of the Day*. I was the proud owner of a Manchester United scarf that I'd knitted myself, with the names of my favourite players emblazoned across in a bold display of my hand-embroidery skills.

With Manchester more than fifty miles from home, it was

too far away to go to watch a football match. More to the point, in an era of mounting tension on the terraces and with football hooliganism rife, I doubt very much my parents would have allowed me to go to watch a first-division side, especially not one with such a big fan base as United. Beatings, stabbings, and fights between rival supporters were unsavoury features of the game in the seventies, and frequently made the headlines.

But I have special memories of the day my mum and dad decided, as a special treat, to take my brother Geoff, also a Man U. supporter, and me to Old Trafford to watch our heroes. The year would, I think, have been 1969. It was a night-time match against Liverpool, and we were mesmerised as we watched George Best weave his special brand of magic on the pitch as the roar of the crowds reached fever pitch. United emerged triumphant, winning 1–0.

After our Man U. adventure, watching Blackpool Football Club seemed a bit tame. However, Bloomfield Road, home of the Seasiders, was not only closer to home, my parents also deemed it to be safer. As a result, I ended up developing a secondary allegiance to the Seasiders (Man U. were still my avowed first love), attending all their home games with my best friend Janice, and her dad.

Blackpool, under the command of Les Shannon and, later, Bob Stokoe, were basking in the glory of being a first-division side, having gained promotion. It meant we got to see all the top teams and star players of the era playing at Bloomfield Road, including Manchester United and the magnificent George Best. Unfortunately, the Seasiders couldn't match the skills of their competitors and were relegated after one sweet but brief season.

There was a real atmosphere at football matches in those days. In 1970, even a relatively low-profile team like Blackpool could command a crowd of thirty thousand spectators. In those days, it was standing room only; you'd stand on the terraces, surrounded by supporters all draped in the distinctive tangerine-and-white colours, and shout and cheer with wild abandon along with the rest of them.

When Janice's dad wasn't able to go to matches, we'd make our own way there, travelling on the number 85 bus to Talbot Road bus station and then catching the distinctive cream-and-green Blackpool Corporation bus to Bloomfield Road. By that point, we would have been little more than thirteen years old, and yet we were given a level of freedom that went way beyond our years. It's a reflection of a world that is vastly different from the one inhabited by today's safety-bubble-wrapped youngsters; it never occurred to our families that we would come to any harm.

Football fever reached a crescendo with the 1970 World Cup finals in Mexico, when England set out to defend their 1966 title. Their quest to repeat that glorious victory was paved with disappointment when they lost to Germany 3–2 in the quarter-finals.

There is a special memory I associate with the 1970 World Cup, and that's buying my first record. It was a recording of the England squad singing 'Back Home', the rousing anthem to the World Cup. I begged and pestered my parents to buy me it. I can still see it now; it was packaged in a plain blue sleeve, bearing the Pye record label. I used to play that record over and over again on the Dansette record player we had in our living room. It was a very catchy anthem, guaranteed to induce patriotic fervour in even the most reluctant of fans.

Following the success of my childhood letter to Prime Minister Harold Wilson, Janice and I decided to try our hand at writing to our football heroes, to see if we could get their autograph. We wrote to former England and Stoke FC goalie Gordon Banks to wish him a speedy recovery when he was seriously injured in a car accident that resulted in the loss of an eye. We were delighted when we received a gracious reply, personally signed by the great man, thanking us for our concerns.

When we wrote to Leeds striker Paul Madeley to say how sorry we were after he'd broken his leg we were rewarded with a nice letter from him, in which he expressed his thanks for our good wishes. Letters to United goalie Alex Stepney and Spurs striker Martin Peters yielded handwritten replies, accompanied by signed photographs. I don't suppose many of today's pampered soccer superstars would take the time or the trouble to send a handwritten thank-you letter – though that might be judging them harshly.

When I wasn't watching football matches, listening to Alexander James Gordon reading the five o'clock football results on the radio on a Saturday afternoon, or reading about the exploits of United in the *Daily Express* or the *Sunday People*, I used to play football. Or to be more accurate, I used to endeavour to create an impression of playing football.

A gang of us, girls and boys, would congregate on the football pitch behind the graveyard at St John's Church – or Jubilee Field, as it was grandly known – after school for a kick-about. We would form ourselves in to mixed-sex, mixed-ability teams. It was all good fun.

However, if I harboured any illusions of being the female equivalent of Roy Mcfarland, I was woefully off the mark. My football skills were only marginally better than my netball skills. I can remember running around the pitch like the proverbial fly in the jam jar, trying to keep my eye on the player I was supposed to be marking – and failing spectacularly. But the important thing for me was during that hour or so of attempting to kick a ball about, I wasn't called names or teased about my appearance. I was one of the gang.

One of my friends at the time, Gill Raby, was a competent player who impressed with her strength and skill. It's perhaps no surprise that her success on the pitch paved the way for an illustrious career as a PE teacher. As for me, well, I achieved a modicum of success as an event organiser, spending hours of my spare time rallying people to play matches at Pilling and Stalmine.

The biggest challenge was making sure there were enough kids available to play on a given Saturday afternoon or a Wednesday, if it was the holidays. It didn't always work that way. Sometimes, if we were short of players, we'd have to resort to a seven-or five-a-side kick-about, or else abandon play altogether. As I look back to those days, I can't help but think that my role as self-appointed organiser of mixed-sex football matches helped to sow the seeds for a later career in project management.

No doubt today, with so many opportunities for organised football, I needn't have gone to this trouble; I could have signed up to a girls' team playing in a properly run women's league. Back then, as I recall, there were no such opportunities for girls to play football; indeed the notion of girls playing at professional or even league level was anathema to a seventies society that regarded football as a masculine pursuit. Those girls who did dribble their way over the boundaries of demarcation between what were widely accepted as male-dominated sports and traditional feminine pursuits, such as tennis or hockey, were perceived, unfairly, as tomboys.

One of the reasons I was gripped by the thrall of football was to gain acceptance among boys as an equal, by playing them at their own game. Perhaps, in my own muddled adolescent thinking, I was trying to strike my blow for women's lib. But somewhere along the way, something else began to tug at me. It was a burning need to express my burgeoning 'girly' side. The driving force for this was dance and fashion, and the dawning of the new disco era.

24

'Let's Dance'

The disco lights are whirling, beaming lurid colours from the low-hung ceiling. A kaleidoscope of blue, pink, purple, and green swirls drift gently across the room. The effect is curiously hypnotic. From the DJ's decks, Edison Lighthouse sing 'Love Grows where My Rosemary Goes', a catchy, if cheesy, song that stormed the hit parade in January 1970, claiming the number-one slot in the charts for five weeks.

On the small wooden dance floor a group of girls, wearing short, floaty dresses with whirls and swirls in almost the same lurid shades as the lights, dance in compact circles, striving to look nonchalant. In the far corner, a group of lads congregate around a table-tennis table pretending to ignore the girls. They're puffing on cigarettes, aiming to look cool. There's a coffee bar, but you can barely hear the clinking of cups above the music. Nearby, there's a pinball machine, emitting strange beeping noises that can be heard above the music.

Cue the next tune: it's Chairmen of the Board singing 'Give Me Just a Bit More Time', a soul song from the Motown label. After this come The Velvelettes with their catchy 'Needle in a Haystack.' Next, the DJ slows the tempo with Jimmy Ruffin's 'Farewell is a Lonely Sound.'

This is Preesall youth club in 1970, an archetypal youth club built to serve the young people in the Over Wyre community. It owed its existence to one man's vision to create a place for young people to go that was safe and theirs to own. Eric Schofield, who always looked to me like a younger version of Eric Morecambe with his dark hair and thick spectacles, was the driving force behind the construction of the single-storey wooden hut on the Lancaster Road playing field that served as the 'hippest' place for Over Wyre teenagers to meet.

Eric wasn't alone in his passion; he had a committee of young people working alongside him. His wife, Jean, and daughter, Pam, also helped out at the meetings. The youth hut was originally built in Poulton and housed the former Poulton social club. Eric and his team of helpers dismantled it and brought it to its new home in Preesall, where it survived for many years before being destroyed by fire.

I nearly didn't go to youth club. All my friends had been to the Tuesday night meetings and were buzzing with excitement at school the day after. My mum was against me going.

'But why?' I demanded. '*Everybody* goes,' I pleaded, my face contorted with anger, hot tears of frustration welling up inside me.

'Who is *everybody*?' my mum demanded.

I persisted. I cried. I stropped. I sulked. In the end, throwing a wobbly paid off. She conceded victory.

'All right, you can go,' she said, grudgingly. 'But I want you to promise me three things: *that you will be ready when we come to pick you up at 9 o'clock prompt; that there will be no smoking; and that under no circumstances will you go outside.*'

Going 'outside' was my parents' euphemism for putting yourself at risk of some greasy-haired lad whisking you behind the toilets for a grope and a fumble, with all its unmentionable risks.

At thirteen, I was innocent and naïve. I knew nothing about teenage pregnancy, and in my unworldly head syphilis was something you grew in your garden. But I knew my parents well enough to understand that if I ever stepped out of the door of that youth hut, my days of going there would be over before they'd even started. I stayed snugly inside.

I enjoyed dancing. There we were, a crowd of us girls dancing dreamily in a circle, handbags in front of us, giggling awkwardly as we moved self-consciously to the beat of Smokey Robinson's 'Tears of a Clown' or Freda Payne's 'Band of Gold'. Back then I was the proud owner of a short pink smock, with a high neckline and long puffed sleeves. It had a pattern of delicate pink flowers, reflecting the era of flower power and psychedelia. Thick white lacy tights completed the look. I thought I was the bee's knees.

I can remember there was one girl who knew how to grab people's attention. Barbara Dawson was three or four years older than me. She was an attractive girl with long, dark flowing hair. She could dance, and she knew it. I can still see her clearing the dance floor as she moved to Tommy James and the Shondell's 'Mony Mony', hips shaking, arms swinging wildly overhead while we all watched, boys as well as girls, open-mouthed with admiration and envy. She was the nearest we had in Preesall to a go-go dancer.

Back then, it was the era of the go-go girl – dancers who knew how to shake their stuff: arms flinging, hips swinging, hair flowing with wild abandon, as epitomised by Pan's People on *Top of the Pops*. And yet, in comparison with the likes of Rhianna, Beyonce and J.Lo, whose sexual posturing and raunchy, gyrating dance routines today seem to verge on the pornographic, it was all innocent somehow. Pan's People might have got your dad's heart racing with their mildly suggestive choreography, but it was all done sweetly and with tongue in cheek.

Going to Preesall youth club wasn't my first foray into the world of youth clubs. A year or so earlier, I'd started going to Pilling youth club. I was just over twelve at the time, the youngest person in the group of thirty or so. Strictly speaking, I shouldn't have been there, because you had to be over thirteen to be a member. But I was allowed in because the person who ran it, Graham Curwen, knew my family. It also helped that I was with a group of friends who were all slightly older than me – my friend, Anne Rossall, her half-cousins, Lynn and Anne Bleasdale, and a few others whose names have faded from memory.

Unlike Preesall youth club, my mum didn't seem to have any qualms about me going to Pilling youth club. Perhaps it was because it was in my home village and she felt there would be less risk of me coming into contact with 'undesirables.' Perhaps it was because she knew Graham and had faith in his ability to organise meetings. Whatever it was, there was never an issue about me going to the meetings at the Oddfellows Hall.

Pilling youth club operated on very similar lines to Preesall youth club, with dancing, table tennis and trips to the ice-skating rink and tenpin bowling. There is a particular memory that stands out for me, and that's of dancing to Bob & Earl's soul classic 'Harlem Shuffle.' Whenever I hear this song, it always takes me back to Pilling youth club. It would have been 1969. There was a kiosk where you could buy a can of pop and a bag of crisps.

Another memory I have is of the time Graham decided to close the youth club early after a crowd began misbehaving. He ordered us all to leave the building. I can't remember what misdemeanours had been committed, but I can recall having to walk home after we'd all been ordered out. My mother was mortified when she discovered what had happened. Luckily for us, it happened during the summer and the lighter evenings, otherwise she would have had something to complain about.

This incident may well have coloured my mother's view of Pilling youth club because I don't remember going much after that. It may well have explained her reluctance to let me go to Preesall youth club and the battle I had to win her over. Back in the seventies, practically every teenager of my age flocked to Preesall youth club, and the tiny hut always seemed to be crowded. There was a real buzz of excitement at school on the day of youth club. It spilt over to the next day as we relived our night out over maths and English lessons. Gossip centred on who had been asked 'out' for a date. Boys, who had been spotty, cheeky little nuisances at twelve, suddenly became eminently fanciable to our rapidly maturing thirteen-year-old minds, as our hormones surged through our gawky bodies.

Being asked out meant you could lay claim to having a boyfriend who would hold your hand in the school playground and kiss you on the school bus. In those days, there was still a sense of innocence and naïvety attached to being a teenager, especially if you were a girl. And perhaps because we lived in a rural backwater we seemed to be more sheltered than teenagers growing up in towns and cities who always appeared to be more streetwise than we were.

Looking back, it's easy to see how the youth club offered a safe rite of passage to our teenage years. It gave us the chance to express ourselves through music, fashions and dance, while cushioned by a soft duvet of safety, in ways that seem lacking today.

As I write this, Preesall youth club faces closure after falling victim to local authority spending cuts. Its demise will doubtless leave a generation of young people with nowhere to go other than to hang around on street corners, which is desperately sad. Back in the seventies, the youth club was about making those all-important tentative steps on the road to maturity, marking a healthy progression to the grown-up world of pubs, discos and nightclubs. It's probably fair to say that without having somewhere to take these baby steps, today's teenagers, girls especially, risk being plunged prematurely into a world for which they are ill-prepared, becoming vulnerable to exploitation.

As well as Preesall youth club, we used to go to the gala dances at Preesall parochial hall. These were organised by the Knott End and Preesall Gala committee, and they had a specific purpose: to choose the 'Knott End and Preesall Gala Queen.' This was a beauty parade, open to all local girls once they had reached their teens.

Halfway through the dance, a dozen or so young women would sashay across the stage in front of a panel of judges, who would decide who should be the next gala queen. There was always lots of excitement over which girl in the bevy of local beauties would be picked for the accolade. And naturally, in true beauty-contest fashion, the winner was almost always overwhelmed with emotion as she picked up her flowers and collected her sash proclaiming her title as 'Gala Queen Elect.' Among the girls, I can remember witnessing being chosen as gala queen over successive gala dances were Susan Butler, Elaine MacPhee, Barbara Dawson and Lorraine Hayes. Long before my time, my Auntie June (Storey) was awarded the regal honour in 1954.

The gala queen contest was played out against a backcloth of national and global beauty competitions. Back then, watching beauty pageants was one of the nation's favourite pastimes, with Miss World and Miss United Kingdom featured among the highlights of the television year, drawing mass audiences and making household names of Eric and Julia Morley, the husband and wife couple who masterminded these contests. Looking back, it seems ludicrous to think of girls being judged solely on the basis on their physical attributes, although there are many who would argue that things haven't really progressed and that women are still treated as objects and judged by their appearances.

After I'd been going to Preesall youth club for a few months, I plucked up the courage to ask my parents if I could go to Stalmine disco. This was held at Stalmine reading room, on Friday evenings. It was a progression from the youth club in that it offered a more 'grown-up' environment. For one thing, it was open to older teenagers and, for another, it was open to young people from outside the area, attracting gangs from as far away as Fleetwood, Poulton and Garstang. And as far as I can remember there were fewer adults present to keep a watchful eye over us.

I fully expected some resistance from my parents but, to my surprise, they agreed to let me go. Again, the same three provisos that had governed my attendance at the youth club were in force. One: be ready to leave promptly at the end of the evening; two: no smoking; and three: no going outside.

The early seventies was the dawn of the new disco movement that swept through the decade with its distinctive rhythmic soul and funk music, dance and fashions. Disco took its name from discothèque, a French term for nightclubs. As the disco craze grew, it became trendy for teenagers to claim they were 'going to the disco', though in reality the word disco became a catch-all term for anywhere that played music and offered dancing.

Stalmine disco, in a draughty village hall, was a world away from Studio 54 and the ultraswish nightclubs of New York and Paris where disco originated. But as far as Over Wyre teenagers were concerned, it was *the* place to go. Young people flocked from far and wide, the mods sweeping in on their scooters, the leather-clad rockers – greasers, as we called them – roaring in to the car park on their Yamahas and Kawasakis, along with those of us who were neither mod nor rocker but somewhere in between.

Back then, teenagers were defined according to their allegiance to a particular group. There were the mods, who dressed neatly in sharp suits, wore their hair short, rode scooters and favoured the music of Tamla Motown, soul and funk. Then there were the rockers, who wore their hair long, rode motorbikes, dressed in leather jackets and jived to the beat of fifties rock 'n' roll.

Mods and rockers weren't a new phenomenon, of course; they were around in the sixties, and volumes have been written on the sociology of youth culture and the clashes between rival gangs. But these neat divisions were an oversimplification and bore little resemblance to what went on in reality, in my experience. Like many of my friends, I was a middle-of-the-roadie who enjoyed the best of both genres. I think a lot of the young people were like that in those days.

At Stalmine disco, the DJ was astute enough to play pop records catering for all tastes. His humble sound system comprised a simple turntable on which to play his vinyl records, accompanied by loudspeakers, microphone and headphones. It was a world away from the high-tech digital sound controls operated by today's DJs, who seem to have enough electronic armoury to pilot an aircraft. Perhaps not surprisingly, compared to the booming disco music of today, the sound quality of the music was poor. Sophisticated it wasn't, but there was something strangely endearing about its simplicity that harks back to a gentler era.

One song I always associate with Stalmine is 'Knock Three Times', a saccharine little number by an American group called Dawn, who had a later hit with 'Tie a Yellow Ribbon Round the Old Oak Tree', coinciding with the return of troops from war-torn Vietnam. Then there was Norman Greenbaum's beaty anthem 'Spirit in the Sky' which always got the leather-clad rockers up and moving. They had their own distinctive style of dancing: feet welded to the floor; hands on hips; body thrusting forwards from the waist; shoulders dipping and swaying in a rhythmic, almost mechanical movement. This was dancing macho style; there was no messing with these guys.

In the midst of all this posturing, a gaggle of us girls would dance demurely in a circle, handbags on the floor, waiting expectantly for a boy to pair up with, hoping for a latter-day Mr Darcy to sweep us off our feet. But those long-haired adolescents clearly hadn't been to Mr Gledhill and Miss Bennett's country dancing lessons, for they knew little about the niceties of inviting a girl to dance. More often than not, it was done wordlessly with a casual shuffle and a sidling towards you, perhaps followed by a nudge and a nod. We girls became adept at picking up the meaning from these non-verbal cues.

As with the youth club, the disco gave us girls the opportunity to get dressed up. I can distinctly remember wearing hot pants, in turquoise velour. They were the skimpiest and tightest of short pants imaginable. These were teamed with a white blouse with long wide sleeves and white imitation leather knee-high boots to complete the ensemble. I was bang on-trend! Back then, everyone was wearing hot pants, in a craze that caught the imagination of the nation. Even my mum had some. Hers were navy blue with a matching bib and shoulder straps. I was mortified. In those days it just wasn't acceptable to have your mum dressing in the same styles as you. She would have been in her mid to late thirties, not even middle-aged, yet in my adolescent eyes she was 'old' – certainly too old for hot pants.

Under the pulsating disco lights our white blouses shone with dazzling brilliance and, embarrassingly for some, the strobe lighting beamed in on white underwear, causing bras to shine iridescently through clothes. Intermittently, the disco lights would be ramped up to send rapid pulsations of white light across the dance floor in dizzying arcs of confusion. Momentarily, you felt disorientated, as if on a fairground ride; then the pulsating would stop and you'd blink your way back to real time and space.

Chairs were arranged around the sides of the room for those who wanted to opt out of the dancing, though most of the lads clustered in gangs, trying to look all macho. Seated in the corners were the courting couples, boys with their arms casually, manfully draped around girls who wore smiles of smug self-satisfaction. These were pre-feminist days (or, at any rate, the discourse of Germaine Greer and her fellow women's libbers had yet to be heard or taken up by the sisters of Stalmine). To hook a boyfriend was the aspiration of every girl, a symbol of womanhood and of acceptance.

It's true to say that some of those couples who met and wooed each other at Stalmine disco went on to become lifelong partners. While it would cause embarrassment to name them all, they included my best friend Anne Rossall who met her husband to be, Peter Bell, at Stalmine. Peter was one of a gang from Garstang who descended on the village. As I write this, Anne and Peter must be approaching their fortieth wedding anniversary.

Though my mum was willing to let me go to Stalmine disco, she would have been horrified by what went on. Inter-gang rivalry sometimes spilt over into fisticuffs and, in the testosterone overflow, boys looked to pick fights with anyone they thought of as threatening. I can remember this happened on one occasion when I was talking to Andrew, the brother of my friend, Vivien. He was a big, stocky lad with a long mane of straggly red hair and matching beard, and he wore a leather jacket. Andrew might have looked menacing, but he was as soft as putty. As we were chatting, without warning a scruffy youth strode over and rammed his motorcycle helmet into his face, for no conceivable reason. I can still see the blood as it gushed from his broken nose and the look of stunned surprise on his face.

I stopped going to Stalmine disco after that, but I don't think it was too long afterwards that the organisers, weary of perpetually breaking up fights, closed the door on disco. But it wasn't the last dance for me and my friends. Later in our teens we started going to the hugely popular village hall dances at Cockerham and St Michael's, venturing into an altogether different world.

25

I (Don't) Think I Love You

Back in the seventies, I was the only girl in the world not to fall head over heels in love with David Cassidy. This fresh-faced teenybopper idol burst on to the pop scene straight from the bosom of the American hit TV show, *The Partridge Family*, with his catchy song 'I Think I Love You.' Millions of teenagers swooned over him, and it was easy to see why. He had lovely crinkly eyes, the most gorgeous smile and a mop of chestnut shoulder-length hair styled in a wispy feather cut. But if I could have changed the words of his chart-topping song they would have been 'I Don't Think I love You.' He was just too sickly-sweet, too pretty-boy angelic for my liking. My friends, who all declared their undying love for Cassidy, couldn't understand my ambivalence.

I was just as unmoved by another American pop idol of the time – Donny Osmond. He made the charts in 1970 with 'Go Away Little Girl.' But he was probably better known for his 1972 smash hit 'Puppy Love', a mushy, slushy ballad that sent teenage girls everywhere into a frenzy of emotion when it was released. Like Cassidy, Osmond – one of a band of Mormon singing brothers, The Osmonds – was too shiny, too spangly, and too squeaky clean for me, with his moonstone teeth and neatly tailored stage suits.

When Rod Stewart stormed into the charts in 1971 with 'Maggie May', I knew I'd found my man. Here he was: spiky hair,

Mr Punch pointy nose, tartan clad, with a rich gravelly voice, twinkly eyes and a mischievous grin. While he wasn't pretty-boy good-looking in the way of Cassidy and Osmond, he had an edginess, a rawness and a sparkle that appealed to me. So, while my friends draped pictures of Cassidy and Osmond over their bedroom walls, I created a shrine to Rod Stewart, staking my claim to him as my own pop hero, and my secret confidant. In the privacy of my bedroom I'd talk to Rod, tell him about my day, confide in him, laugh with him. Naturally, he didn't respond, other than to grin inanely, tam-o'-shanter perched jauntily atop his head. But it was enough to know he was there, waiting for me at the end of each day.

Back then, as today with the likes of One Direction and Justin Beiber pressing the fantasy buttons of today's starry-eyed teenagers, there was a cult of pop superstardom and teenage hero worship. And where better to read about the antics of Rod, or Dave, or Donny – as well as pick up a full-page poster of your idol – than in *Jackie* magazine?

Like millions of girls, I devoured *Jackie*, reading it from cover to cover every week when it plopped through the letter box each Thursday, costing three-and-a-half pence. *Jackie* contained everything you needed to know about pop stars, fashions and make-up, as well as offering advice on boyfriends and how to deal with your parents, siblings or best friends. There was always a cartoon-strip story, highlighting dilemmas faced by the characters – for example, there's a girl who really fancies her brother's best friend. But he has a girlfriend already. What is a girl to do? You could trust *Jackie* to guide you through this moral conundrum.

Jackie also featured sage advice on how to develop a career. As an exercise in nostalgia, I was able to buy a 1971 edition on the internet. Joy of joys, it contained a special feature on 'Getting the Glamour Jobs: No 1 Private Secretary'. It describes how girls could earn a four-figure salary of up to £1500 by working as a private secretary. The article highlights the story of one girl who topped up her two years at secretarial college with a 'grooming course' at the Lucie Clayton school of modelling, as the route to her career. It speaks volumes about how restricted seventies girls were in terms of career expectations and aspirations, and how good looks and good grooming were equated with career success. Twenty years on, and girls of my generation still weren't that far removed from the notions of the fifties housewife that beset our mothers' generation.

The part of *Jackie* I liked best was the Cathy and Claire problem page. Cathy and Claire were like two friendly big sisters who dispensed sensible, kindly advice and offered words of wisdom and reassurance to quell any form of teenage angst. They'd gently advise you what to do if a boyfriend got overamorous and caution you against 'going too far.' They'd offer you words of comfort after a stinging row with your parents or best friend. But, most of all, they helped you to realise that your own problems, no matter how trivial or how severe, were likely to be shared by countless other teenagers throughout the land. In their own way, Cathy and Claire were a lifeline for teenagers, dealing with issues you might not like to talk about with your parents or friends. Certainly, they were a major influence on my teens, shaping how I thought and behaved.

26

'You Wear It Well'

I can remember poring over *Jackie's* fashion and make-up pages, picking up tips on the latest trends. The seventies were an exciting time for fashion-conscious teenagers, with a bewildering choice of styles, from the skimpiest of miniskirts and hot pants, to midiskirts and floaty dresses, all in bright colours. And who could forget bell-bottomed trousers – wide-legged pants that flared from below the knee? Or those platform shoes that you would teeter on vertiginously, as you endeavoured to look cool while desperately trying not to collapse in an ungainly heap on the floor? I remember buying a button-through midiskirt in chocolate brown and teaming this with a chiffon blouse with an orange-and-brown geometric design. My pleasure in this purchase was short-lived when my mum commented that I looked 'droopy.' By this, I think she meant the skirt's elongated shape didn't do me any favours. It was enough to send me racing to my bedroom for one of my, by now, habitual sulks.

Between the ages of thirteen and fourteen, I was allowed off the parental leash to go to Blackpool with my friends on the number 85 Ribble bus. We'd spend hours just browsing round the fashion shops. One of the coolest places to visit was Chelsea Girl, in Bank Hey Street, with its dark, enticing interior, lively music and iconic red heart motif. But we were just as enthralled by C&A which, in those days, seemed to cater well for fashion-conscious teenagers on a careful budget.

Back then, lots of independent boutiques and fashion shops dotted the resort, creating a real fashion buzz that would rival any of the bigger cities. Among these were Carley's Continental Fashions in Birley Street and, some time later, a boutique called 'Av a Butchers, which became my favourite shop for its quirky, original designs. Sometimes, we would peek through the windows of Diana Warren, the high-class designer shop boasting top-of-the-range-fashions, but we never ventured into its sleek interior, aware that our grubby teenage hands would be frowned on. Shoe shops abounded: Dolcis, Freeman, Hardy and Willis, and Blackpool's own Vernon Humpage, each bedecked with a dizzying array of platform-soled shoes and boots, with heels that would defy gravity.

It was from the enticing rails of Chelsea Girl that I bought my first tank top. Tank tops were knitted jumpers without sleeves. They seemed to blossom in every fashion shop. Mine was a chunky V-necked top, with its fancy knitted pattern featuring blue and green diamond shapes. I wore this over a white long-sleeved blouse, though you could go the whole hog and remain sleeveless. With black bell-bottomed trousers and platform shoes to complete the ensemble, I was ready to hit the world or, at the very least, the youth clubs and dance halls of Over Wyre.

I was also the proud owner of a Ben Sherman shirt, the long, classically tailored shirt with its trademark full back pleat, long sleeves and button-down collar, favoured by the mods and, later, the new skinhead movement. Mine came in brown-and-beige gingham. By then, skinheads had started to make their appearance in our village, stomping around in their bovver boots and braces, oozing attitude. I can remember there was a female skinhead, Sandra Sweetman; with her short, cropped hair and Doc Martens, she looked like someone you definitely wouldn't want to get on the wrong side of!

As seventies teenagers, we were spared the bothersome tasks of messing about with stockings and suspenders, or fiddling with the panty girdles that beset our mothers' generation: we had tights! Tights were seen as liberating, easy to wear and time-saving for a whole new generation of women beginning to find liberation in other spheres of life, including work and, with the advent of the pill, sexual freedom.

One of the big problems with tights, back then, was they seemed to ladder easily, and were too costly to replace. Like many of my generation, I can remember dabbing my tights with a generous dollop of nail varnish in an attempt to stop an unsightly ladder in its tracks. We girls must have looked a sight – legs encased in flattering figure-hugging hosiery, studded with blobs of pearlised pink nail varnish.

Every Saturday my parents gave my brother and me sixpence each as pocket money. This became known in our household as the 'Saturday Sixpence.' It was a token amount, and nowhere near enough to meet my desire to be taken seriously as a pop and fashion princess. Back then, as today, it was common for kids to earn themselves a bit of money by doing a paper round or getting some other kind of part-time job. I was no exception, begging my mum incessantly to allow me to work. I would have been about fourteen when she finally caved in to my demands to let me have a Saturday job working in a shop.

Hallett's, in the Stakepool district of Pilling, was a busy shop, an Aladdin's cave, filled to the rafters with DIY products, electrical appliances, gardening implements and household goods. If I close my eyes, I can still picture the store. It had a wooden-fronted facade and you had to climb steps to reach the entrance. To the right of the door, the wall was lined with shelves containing rows of paint, stacked up neatly like soldiers on parade, one row for white gloss, one for undercoat, and so on. Nearby were lawnmowers, electric and motor operated, in an assortment of shapes and sizes. Opposite these, shelves groaned with household appliances – kettles, toasters, food mixers ... Towards the back of the building, drawers and shelves bulged with nuts, bolts, nails and screws of every size and shape imaginable. But what I can remember most is the pervasive smell, an intoxicating chemical mixture of paraffin, paint, and new plastic – mingled with Mrs Hallett's exotic perfume.

Mr Hallett was a softly spoken gentle bear of a man. Mrs Hallett, her dark hair done up in a neat bun, was noted for her very short skirts and white knee-high boots, drawing admiring glances from her many male customers and it's probably fair to say she attracted many more shoppers because of this.

When I applied for the job there as Saturday assistant, I imagined I'd be presiding over a counter, making polite and cheerful conversation to customers as I served them tins of peach-coloured paint or advised them of the benefits of non-stick baking tins. My illusions were quickly dispelled on my first morning there.

'Now, Angela,' said Mr Hallett in his fatherly voice. 'What I'd like you to do this morning is tidy up these paint shelves.' It didn't take me long to realise this involved making sure paint tins were stacked in neat, orderly rows along the shelves, ensuring no wayward tins of emulsion had wandered into the territory occupied by the non-drip gloss.

'That looks much better,' Mr Hallett remarked after I'd spent an hour or so shuffling paint tins around. 'And now I have another little job for you. You're in charge of the bacon butties, and I want you to go to the shop and get some for us to eat at break time,' he said, proffering a pencil and brown paper bag for me to write the order down.

So this was, more or less, my job role: general tidy-upper, sweeper of the lino floor, duster of the shelves, delver among the boxes of nails and screws to make sure these were well stocked up, and – as befitted my junior status – making sure Mr and Mrs Hallett (and their shop assistant, a girl who, though only a couple of years older than me, had managed to pick the plum role of counter assistant) were kept well supplied with tea, toast, and bacon sandwiches, the latter purchased from neighbouring Ireton's store.

There was one more duty that Mr Hallett assigned to me, and that was to organise the outdoor displays, designed to entice customers to his shop. Displays took on a seasonal theme, and during the summer there would be a row of gleaming green lawnmowers of varying shapes and sizes – from cumbersome Flymos to dainty, electrically operated mowers – lined up along the front of the shop. Next to these would be an array of brightly striped sunloungers, fold-up garden chairs, and canopies. Alongside these would be a selection of spades, hoes and hedge cutters.

Arranging the display became my pride and joy, but it involved a great deal of physical exertion. It meant dragging the lawnmowers from inside the shop and heaving them down the steps to their allotted space outside. It was no job for a slip of a young girl, and there's no doubt it would have put a frown on the faces of today's health and safety inspectors. But back in the seventies nobody thought of this as an issue, least of all my parents.

Working in Hallett's hardware shop wasn't the most glamorous job for a girl aspiring to the finer things in life, but it provided me with enough money to buy records and clothes. I can't remember how much I received for my first wage. But I can recall the first record I purchased with my hard-earned cash. It was 'Chirpy Chirpy Cheep Cheep' by a Scottish group called Middle of the Road, released in 1971; a catchy, if silly, song.

I seem to remember it costing about seven shillings to buy a record.

27

'Puppy Love'

During the winter months at Hallett's, I was assigned an additional role: that of paraffin dispenser. This meant ladling paraffin oil from a metal vat into smaller containers which customers purchased to use as fuel for their heaters. It was dirty, smelly, oily work, and a world away from the glamour of the shop assistant's role I had envisioned. But it had its compensations: there were some boys who used to stay at nearby Fold House Caravan Park, and if they spied me working outside they'd stop off at the hardware shop for a chat as they strolled past. One of them, a dark-haired George Best lookalike (well, to my young eyes he was) called Paul Frost, with gentle brown eyes and gorgeous gap-toothed smile, took a shine to me. Eventually, he asked me to go out with him.

He lived in Manchester, but visited the caravan with his parents each weekend during the summer. We used to meet up after I'd finished work (after I'd got myself changed and dolled up) and we'd go out for a walk, strolling along the lanes, his arms wrapped around me proprietorially, or visit the Verona cinema in Knott End. When the caravan park closed during the winter months, we kept in touch by writing long letters to each other, mainly about football, for he was a Man U. fan, like me. It was hardly full-blown lust, more a gentle romance founded on the soft, marshmallow sweetness of youthful innocence.

One wet Saturday in November, as I was tidying some tins

of paint at the front of the shop, hair straggly and wet because I'd been outside in the rain to get some paraffin from another building for a customer, I saw Paul out of the corner of my eye, his face peering at me shyly through the window like an apparition in the soft rain. He'd travelled all the way from Manchester by bus just to see me on my birthday. I would have been fourteen then, and he not much older.

Later, as we cuddled up in a telephone kiosk, rain pattering against the windows, me reeking of paraffin, he produced a tiny gift-wrapped parcel. Inside the box was a cheap necklace with a faux emerald stone, yet if I'd been Elizabeth Taylor, dripping in diamonds, I wouldn't have been any happier than at that moment. Here I was, in the soft and tender throes of my own 'puppy love.' Alas, distance and the absence of any way of maintaining meaningful contact, other than by letter – with social media still two generations away – meant our love missives became shorter, with longer gaps between them. By spring, and the start of the new caravan season, we'd drifted apart.

28

'Saturday Night at the Movies'

In between youth club, discos and schoolwork, we still found time to go to the Verona Cinema, Knott End's small family cinema, run with a steely hand by its owners, the redoubtable Mr and Mrs Miller. Just as the tiny cinema building had served in my parents' era, it still played a big part in the social scene of teenagers of my generation. And it wasn't just a case of 'Saturday Night at the Movies', but just about every night at the movies. This wonderful little cinema, housed in what is now The Squash, offered enough variety of entertainment to keep people enthralled most nights of the week.

I can remember going to see many of the top films there during the seventies. Who could forget *Love Story*, a weepie starring Ryan O'Neal and Ali MacGraw as a couple whose love is doomed when Ali MacGraw develops leukaemia? It was definitely a film you needed to take your hankies to. Other films I can remember watching were *Oliver* starring Jack Wild, and James Bond in *Diamonds are Forever*, with Shirley Bassey belting out the theme tune. Then there was *Buona Sera, Mrs Campbell*, a quirky comedy starring Italian siren Gina Lollobrigida.

And the great thing about having our very own cinema on the doorstep was it meant our parents had no qualms about letting us go. Whereas they would have baulked at the idea of us catching a bus to Blackpool in the evening to see the latest offerings at the ABC or Odeon, the Verona was seen as reassuringly safe, a place where we were unlikely to encounter gangs of marauding knife-wielding skinheads or undesirables seeking to take advantage of impressionable young girls. What's more, the films nearly always ended in time to catch the last bus home to Pilling.

Mr Miller, the projectionist, would generally hover in the background. It was the formidable Mrs Miller who was the public face of the Verona, issuing tickets and taking orders for refreshments: tea, coffee, soft drinks or ice cream. I can remember her as a straight-talking, no-nonsense character who you wouldn't want to get on the wrong side of. It's probably fair to say that's how most people of my generation thought of her.

At the front of the cinema was a small foyer with a booking office. The main auditorium was downstairs and there was a single row of seats in the upstairs balcony. Back-row seats were taken up by courting couples clinched in passionate embraces, slobbering all over each other, heedless of the story being played out on the big screen. Was I ever one of these? My lips are sealed; there are some things a lady doesn't tell, even when she is writing her own life story! Suffice to say there were those who, when asked to recall key moments from their film, were hard-pressed to remember any. Clearly, their minds and mouths were otherwise engaged.

Something strange happens on one of my cinema visits. Here I am, one cold winter Saturday evening with three friends. We're looking forward to watching S.W.A.L.K. (Sealed with a Loving Kiss), a soppy rite-of-passage story starring teenybopper icons Jack Wild and Mark Lester. As the lights dim and the film starts, I settle into my seat. The room is warm and a feeling of fuzzy drowsiness envelopes me. The images on the screen flicker and fade, reappear, flicker and fade again. My eyes feel heavy and I feel myself sliding into the soft cushion of sleep. As I drift away, images of sharp-suited, grinning Bill Haley and the

Comets belting out their jaunty 'Rock Around the Clock' appear on the screen, incongruously.

The next thing I notice is that the cinema seats have been moved back and the whole floor has opened out in to a glittering dance hall. People are locking arms, doing the jive, dancing frenetically like there's no tomorrow: Teddy boys in drainpipes and winkle-pickers sporting DA haircuts; girls in full-skirted dresses and flouncy petticoats. And the whole building is shaking to the rock 'n' roll beat.

I've been transported back to the Verona of the fifties, when the cinema doubled up as a vibrant dance hall on Saturday nights. But this wasn't a dream; it really happened. In reality I have no recollection of those days as they were before my time, but plenty of others have. My Auntie June is among those who can remember how the Verona became a magnet for rock 'n' roll aficionados from across the district. The young folk would cycle to Knott End from the neighbouring villages, leaning their bicycles at the side of the cinema.

'We had a great time,' recalls June. 'And the place was packed out. It was *the* place to go. People would cycle home and they'd still be buzzing with excitement.'

In keeping with the rock 'n' roll theme, the cinema boasted an American-style cafe to the right of the main entrance, selling hot drinks and Wall's ice cream. It featured a cafe bar made up of stacked Wall's ice cream tins designed to reflect the fifties movie-scene ambience.

But, popular though the rock 'n' roll nights were, the Verona's main purpose was as a thriving little cinema, serving the local community. Don Stringfellow can recall the ritual of queuing to see films in the fifties.

'You used to go in to the foyer, get your tickets, order your coffee and biscuits, go outside, up the fire exit steps, and you entered the auditorium through a curtain,' he remembers. 'Upstairs there was the balcony. All of the back-row seats were double seats, which meant they were handy for courting couples. There were always two films, and during the interval Mrs Miller would bring round our tea and coffee, which cost extra. At the interval she would stand at the front and shout, "Hands up who ordered these drinks!"'

A cinema programme kept by Don Stringfellow from 1964 provides a fascinating glimpse in to the films of the era. Cinema patrons certainly got value for their money, for more often than not they got to see two films for the price of one ticket. On the week beginning 3 August 1964, Over Wyre cinemagoers could look forward to a screening of *On the Beat* starring Norman Wisdom, followed by Charles Drake in *No Name on the Bullet,* both on the same night.

Not only that, but films were changed at the beginning, middle and end of the week, which meant there was always plenty of variety. It speaks volumes of the popularity of cinemagoing back then and how it gave people an opportunity to get dressed up, go out, meet people, and find romance.

Sadly, in my view, today's uber-modern, technically advanced but coldly impersonal multiplexes seem to lack the charm and authenticity of the traditional cinema. I can't help but wonder what Mr and Mrs Miller would have made of brash present-day multiscreen complexes such as Vue and Odeon.

When the Verona closed, sometime during the mid seventies, many Over Wyre folk mourned its sad demise, myself included. It was somewhere you could go with your friends and have a good time. It was an unforgettable part of Knott End's vibrant youth scene back in the swinging sixties and sizzling seventies, a culture that has since been swept aside by the tidal wave of demographic change brought about by a shift towards an increasingly ageing population.

The irony is that we who were part of that generation of bright young kids are now growing old, alongside the folk who have been lured to Knott End over the past fifty years or so by its forest of purpose-built retirement bungalows.

29

'Riding Along on my Pushbike, Honey'

Every Saturday I used to cycle the mile or so from our house to Hallett's, and I'd bike home for lunch, returning to work in the afternoon. Back then, most of my friends had bicycles and we were far less reliant on our parents for lifts than today's generation.

When I wasn't working at Hallett's, I used to help my friend Janice to do her evening paper round and we'd cycle to houses and farms lying on the perimeter of the village, thrusting *The Evening Gazette* or *The Lancashire Evening Post* through letter boxes – but not before we'd had the chance to peek through the football reports first.

My standard-issue Raleigh bike, bought for me by my parents for my birthday, had a navy blue frame and came with a wicker basket attached to the handle bars. As bikes go, it was nothing fancy, and certainly nothing like the Chopper – those strange-looking squat bikes with funny squashed-up frames, fat, chunky wheels, and high handlebars that seemed to be all the rage in the seventies. But my trusty Raleigh gave me the freedom to go out with friends, to shop and to go to the pictures – in short, to go wherever I wanted.

During the school holidays, between going out after breakfast and getting back before tea, the days stretched out before us, the hours full of anticipation and youthful energy and exuberance.

Virtually every day I used to cycle the three or so miles to the tiny hamlet of Eagland Hill with my friend Janice. We would visit the cottage home of Janice's former neighbour, a kindly elderly lady who had taken on the role as a sort of adopted grandmother to Janice. She'd cook us chips and bacon on her home range – big fat, chunky chips and the thickest slab of bacon you've ever seen. Sometimes we used to stay over at her cosy little cottage with its low-beamed ceilings, whispering in to the night our hopes and dreams, and sharing girlish gossip and stories. Janice succeeded Anne Rossall as my best friend and people often used to comment that we looked alike. Often Janice would find herself being called 'Angela' and I would find myself answering to 'Janice.'

We'd think nothing of pedalling six miles or so to Hambleton, to the home of another friend, Enid. From there, we'd catch the number 85 bus in to Blackpool in order to look around the shops. Or we'd cycle to Knott End to catch the ferry boat across to Fleetwood. I can recall going into Hogg's Fashion Shop, on Lord Street, and coming out with a crisp white cotton blouse with daring lace-up front and thinking I was the queen of fashion.

It sounds a cliché but back then you really did feel as if you had the freedom to stay out all day long without your parents worrying where you had got to. My mum knew I could be relied upon to return home at around six o'clock in time for tea. Like Pavlov's famous salivating dogs, I could sniff out food from miles away.

We didn't have mobile phones in those days, of course, but somehow life was much safer and gentler, and the roads were quieter. That's not to say my parents didn't drill into me the importance of not getting into a car with strangers. And it isn't to say there weren't perverts lurking around our narrow country lanes. I can remember being stopped when riding my bike along Backsands Lane, Pilling, by a blond bouffant-haired chancer in an estate car asking me if I wanted to go for a drive with him.

He was staying at a nearby caravan park. He was improbably good-looking and seemed plausible, as far removed from the stereotypical image of an oily, unkempt 'stranger' as you could imagine. My mum's warnings ringing in my ears, I resisted, but I still shudder when I think of what might have happened if I'd got into that car with him.

One of the other pitfalls of riding your bike along Pilling's narrow lanes was an encounter with the village bobby, PC Ted Norris. Each village had its own resident police officer, based in the local police house. Ted was happily ensconced in Pilling police house with his wife and large family. He was an easy-going and popular bobby, who ruled with a light touch, preferring to issue miscreants with a gentle warning rather than produce his summons book. But he had two pet hates, and both related to cyclists: he hated kids riding their bikes without lights, and he hated them riding without having their hands firmly planted on the handlebars – or riding 'with no hands' as we called it.

As accomplished cyclists, we became adept at riding our bikes with no hands – cycling along at speed with our arms placed casually by our sides, relying entirely on leg power to keep us in balance. It was a risky business and, rightly, Ted was concerned for our safety. Fearful of erring on the wrong side of the law, we would take great pains to ensure that whenever we were in the vicinity of the police station we rode our bikes with our hands firmly affixed to the handlebars, only releasing them when we thought we were safely out of sight.

But there was one occasion when he caught us out. We were riding along Taylor's Lane, cockily racing along without hands on handlebars, when Ted pulled up in front of us in his pale blue Panda car.

'Use your hands!' he commanded, as he wound down the window. 'And if I catch you riding without hands again I'll tell your parents.'

I can remember blushing a furious crimson. Police officers,

just like doctors and teachers, were authority figures and you wouldn't dream of challenging them. Being told off by a police officer was enough to make you want to crawl away with shame and embarrassment. I felt I'd been caught in the act of some heinous crime.

When you did as much cycling as I did, punctured tyres occurred on an almost daily basis. Under my grandad's tutelage, I learnt how to mend a puncture using a bucket of water to locate the tiny holes or tears in the inner tube. But it was a tiresome chore and sometimes it was easier to take my bike to Harry Melling's to be repaired. Harry ran a bicycle repair shop from a cabin behind his bungalow in Taylor's Lane. It was a veritable treasure trove, with inner tubes festooned from the ceiling, wheels slung across the floor, bicycle pumps littering the workbench, along with a whole panoply of cycling paraphernalia – oily chains, nuts and bolts, dismembered seats and handlebars. Harry was an acknowledged expert on bicycle repairs locally, a title he shared with his twin brother Charlie, who ran an almost identical business from his home in Hallgate Lane, Preesall.

If you ever ran into any kind of difficulty while out on your bike, you always knew you were never more than ten minutes away from a telephone kiosk. The bright red phone booths emblazoned with the Crown insignia were a familiar and reassuring presence in our rural community in those pre mobile-phone days. Dotted along the lanes at intervals of half a mile or so, they were a welcoming sight if you needed to contact your parents or arrange a rendezvous with your friends.

Inside each kiosk was a mounted handset with two buttons: an 'A' button and a 'B' button. You lifted the handset, dialled the number and inserted your money. If the person answered, you pressed the 'A' button, which would allow your call to proceed. If there was no answer, you pressed the 'B' button to get your coins back (and sometimes you would be rewarded with a bonanza, collecting someone else's coins as well as your own!). Charges were set according to geography; I think the minimum charge for a local call was 2p, with more for longer calls.

Without any form of air ventilation, telephone booths were hot, stuffy and often smelly, reeking of a noxious mix of cigarette smoke, body odour and, sometimes, alcohol. Kiosks were always a handy rendezvous point for courting couples (as I'd already discovered in my meetings with Paul Frost), provided you ignored the irate old man in a flat cap tapping on the window, mouthing at you to clear off out so he could use the phone, or the cheeky little kids puckering their hot breathy lips against the glass panels, in imitation of your kissing.

There are still a few old-fashioned red telephone kiosks scattered around Knott End and Preesall and neighbouring Hambleton, though one or two look forlorn and in desperate need of some TLC. But it's sad to see how, in some villages, kiosks have vanished altogether, or been replaced by modern, featureless glass kiosks with drab grey panels. Pilling has some of these later kiosks, located around the village. They may blend more readily into the environment, but it's fair to say they lack the cheery charm and quintessentially English character of the red kiosk. It was a mystery to me why Knott End and Preesall have kept their red kiosks, while near-neighbour Pilling has opted for the newer versions. I spoke to our local councillor, Vivien Taylor, who told me that Knott End and Preesall had retained their red kiosks at the behest of the local council. Mystery solved!

Living in such close proximity to the sea, we became sea orphans, whiling away lazy days on the beach. We'd cycle to the beach at Fluke Hall, taking a bottle of pop and a bag of crisps with us and happily spend an afternoon playing rounders or riding out to the wreck. This was the remains of a ship, landed a mile and a half or so off the coast, the wooden planks of the hull jutting out from the sand like a row of uneven teeth. For me, those rotting remains, peeping out from the sticky, oily sand, whispered their own mysteries of lives lost to merciless sea storms.

Pilling Sands, calm and benign on warm, balmy summer days, take a malevolent turn on storm-tossed winter nights when high tides whip up the waves and nature vents her full fury on the landscape. Historical records are full of accounts of ships that have fallen foul of angry storms or fast-flowing waters and met their untimely end on Pilling Sands. On our trips to the wreck we used to tell stories to each other, imagining what kind of tragedies had befallen the unfortunates who found themselves washed up at Pilling.

'Could it have been a pirate called Jim, with a big black cat?' I mused to my friend Janice.

'And his young mate called Bill, on his first voyage and feeling very sea sick,' she added.

And on and on we would go, feeding our imagination with stories of the sea until it was nearly possible to believe them to be true.

One of the big attractions of the summer months was the motorcycle sand races on Pilling Sands. Bikers from far and wide would descend on our tiny community to compete in the thrills and spills of the sand races, organised by the Fleetwood and District Motorcycle Club. Back then, motorcycle speedway was a hugely popular sport, and the flat, wide expanse of the beach made a perfect sand racing circuit.

I can remember cycling to Fluke Hall with friends to watch these races, and being caught up in the excitement of it all: the ear-splitting noise of a dozen or more mighty machines revving in chorus, tearing across the beach to leave a golden cloud-storm of sand in their wake; the breathless chatter of the commentator over the public address system; the macho smell of oil carried on the air by the soft sea breezes; the cheers and applause from the crowd as the winner smashed home.

The races attracted spectators and competitors from all over the north west, and among the racers was Pilling's own speed king Geoff Cornthwaite. But as far as my friends and I were concerned, we weren't really interested in who won the main prizes. No, we were interested in one thing only: boys! And in this masculine of sports, there were lots of them, leather-jacketed, budding young Steve McQueens. It was definitely the place to see and be seen. We'd stroll around, somewhat precociously dressed in short skirts and knee-high boots, trying to cultivate an air of cool nonchalance. If we hoped to catch the eye of some lad, then we were invariably disappointed – for the boys were only interested in one thing, and that was the motorbikes, their eyes focused on the dusty track with rapt attention.

The Pilling sand races ended some time during the mid seventies after the popularity of speedway racing dwindled. There's no doubt the activity would have been frowned on by today's health and safety police, on the basis of its dangers to spectators due to lack of adequate barriers. But back then it all seemed great fun.

Today motorbikes still play a big part in the Knott End community. Every Wednesday evening during the summer months hundreds of bikers roar in to the village, congregating at Knott End cafe where, over a bacon butty and a cup of tea, they can exchange biking stories and admire each other's sleek Hondas, BMWs, Yamahas and Suzukis. Some of these are born-again bikers, who are no doubt keen to reminisce on the heady days of the motorbiking sixties and seventies epitomised in iconic films such as *Easy Rider*. I wonder if they ever talk about Pilling sand races and those long-forgotten days when the beach was transformed into a speedway circuit?

30

'Rock Me Baby'

In the autumn of 1971, my parents summoned my brother and me to a meeting in our living room. They had something to tell us.

'You're going to have a new brother or sister,' said my mum. At thirty-eight, she was pregnant with her third child. I was approaching fifteen by this time and totally bemused and perplexed. It just wasn't a cool thing to tell your friends your mum was having a baby. There I was, in my own self-absorbed little teenage world, obsessing about boys, fashion, and music, not to mention grappling with the burden of schoolwork and thinking about my own future and career. Hadn't I enough to contend with, without having to deal with the impending change to family dynamics that a squalling new baby would inevitably bring?

My mum kept reasonably well throughout her pregnancy, although I think she was often tired. Not only did she have one very obstreperous teenager to manage – me – along with my brother, who though less truculent was quietly burrowing his own way through teenage angst, she was also busy helping my dad with his joinery business. Over the months that followed, I tried to ignore her growing bump and the evidence of this new little life inside her.

On 4 April 1972, my dad took me to watch Preston North End play in an evening match at Deepdale, their home ground.

I can't remember who they played, or the final score, but that evening was memorable for two reasons. Firstly, a fan was stabbed. This was in the days when violence on the terraces between rival fans was still rife. I can still see this young supporter walking in front of me, helped by a first aider, a knife protruding from his shoulder, rivulets of blood trickling down his shirt. Secondly, as we arrived home we noticed my mum wasn't there but my grandma was. She told us my mum had started her labour pains and Grandad Bill had taken her to the Royal Lancaster Infirmary. My dad's face registered instant panic and he sped off to the hospital as fast as his joinery van would allow him.

That night I went to bed and I must have slept, because some time early the next morning I can remember my dad coming in to my bedroom. 'You've got a baby sister,' he said.

The new baby, when she arrived home, was a cute little thing with thick, dark hair, and I grew to love her, my initial misgivings at having a baby in the house evaporating virtually overnight. My mum used to let me wind her and I became a dab hand at rubbing her back, aiding her to emit big gassy burps, though I drew a line at nappy changes. When it came to deciding on names, I suggested Karen because it reminded me of a girl at school who was popular with all her classmates – Karen Johnson, that girl I'd once accidentally nearly knocked out cold during school netball. Karen was a cool name; it smacked of schoolgirl niceness but it had a hint of seventies trend. So that was it: Karen it was. Or Karen Linda, to be precise, my mum and dad having chosen the Linda bit.

With a baby in the house and a business to run, my mum insisted on me helping around the house. I used to assist with the washing-up, preparing the vegetables, and the cleaning, until she eventually saw the wisdom of employing a cleaner. It's funny: as I look back, I don't ever remember my brother being asked to do these things. There was still a clear demarcation in roles for boys and girls in those days, with girls expected to fulfil domestic duties. I can remember feeling a simmering resentment at having to help around the house, but I was probably no different from any of my friends who had the same expectations heaped on them.

31

'Making Your Mind Up'

I was one of the 'ROSLA' generation of secondary kids – the last to have the option of leaving school at fifteen. The government introduced the raising of the school leaving age (ROSLA) in 1972, and this took effect the following year. It meant that from 1973 it was compulsory for all pupils to stay on at school until they reached sixteen. Although we could leave school at fifteen, in reality most pupils opted to stay on an extra year, preferring to leave with a clutch of GCE O levels, or CSEs (Certificate of Secondary Education), rather than coming away from school empty-handed, as they would have done if they'd left a year earlier.

GCE O levels were the standard qualification, but those who were less able had the option of taking CSEs, which were less stringent. A top-grade CSE counted as an O-level equivalent. Some pupils, myself included, took a combination of GCEs and CSEs. This meant that you had a safety valve in case, for example, you failed your GCE in maths; at least there was a chance you might gain a high-scoring CSE in the same subject.

Now in my fourth year at St Aidan's, I had two years of formal education left. At this point, teachers began murmuring to us about our careers, urging us to think about what we wanted to do after leaving school. As secondary modern kids in the seventies, our career aspirations were never particularly high. Girls were generally expected to go into secretarial or shop work when they left school; boys were encouraged to seek an apprenticeship in a trade such as joinery, motor vehicle maintenance, or electrical engineering. Back then, jobs and opportunities for apprenticeships abounded. Living in a rural area meant there were also opportunities to work on farms or in rural businesses, and several of my classmates left school knowing they had a guaranteed job and future within their family business.

Occasionally, girls aspired to careers in teaching or nursing, and boys dreamt of joining the fire service or police force, but it's probably fair to say they tended to be the exception rather than the rule. Parents were often a strong influence on career choices. My parents were no different; they had a career in teaching mapped out for me, though I was less convinced of this as the choice for a glittering future.

'It's a good job for a woman,' my mum would say. 'It pays well and you get long holidays – ideal for when you come to have your own children, because you can be at home with them in the holidays.'

I was less convinced by this argument, but it seemed there was a conspiracy involving my mum, my teachers and the careers advisor to force me into becoming a teacher. Careers advice in those days was scant, but I can recall being called in to a meeting with the local authority careers advisor and my mum. Mr Gledhill, who was the boys' PE teacher, was also in the meeting. I think this must have been because he was also head of the fifth year and had responsibility for careers.

Our conversation went something like this:

Careers advisor: 'So, Angela, what would you like to do when you leave school?'

Me: 'Well ... I thought about journalism. I'm good at English and I like writing stories.'

It was true: I was and I did.

Mr Gledhill: 'To be a journalist you have to be pushy and outgoing, and you have to have a thick skin. I think you're too quiet and gentle for that. Have you thought about teaching?'

Mum: 'Yes, we've talked about teaching. I think it's something that would suit Angela – and it's a good job for a woman to go into.'

Me: 'I thought about fashion design ...'

It was true: I loved clothes and fashion and I enjoyed art and considered myself to be arty.

Careers advisor (shaking his head): 'It's a very competitive career, very hard to get into. And you have to be exceptional in order to make the big time.'

Mr Gledhill: 'Have you thought about teaching?'

Mum: 'Yes, it would be a really rewarding job to go into, a career for life.'

So that was it. My future was decided. I wouldn't be leaving school at sixteen. I'd be staying on to take A levels in religious studies and home economics (the only subjects on offer at A level at St Aidan's for those wishing to extend their education). My A levels would be the passport to a place at Breck Road teacher training college in Poulton.

A discussion followed on which subjects I would need to take at GCE and CSE level. Satisfied, the careers advisor put down his pen and looked up at my mum and me, signalling our session was drawing to a satisfactory close.

'Do you have any more questions, Angela?' he asked.

'Er, yes ... what do you need to do in order to become a police lady?'

With that, there was a collective groan from the careers advisor, Mr Gledhill and my mum.

'You would need to be tough, quick-thinking and used to thriving under pressure, and you're too meek and sensitive,' said Mr Gledhill dismissively.

The fact that these same words might also have applied to teaching seemed to have escaped his notice. I left the careers interview with a sinking feeling in my stomach, a sense that the rest of my life had been laid out in front of me in monochrome grey. There was nothing wrong with teaching, as such. It just felt, to my idealistic fifteen-year-old self, that it lacked the allure, the sparkle, the flashing bright lights and fizz of journalism or fashion design.

Though I was disappointed with the way the careers interview had gone, I was determined to work hard at school, get good O-level and CSE results and carve out my own career pathway. Following the careers interview, teachers arranged for me to take O levels in English language, history, geography, human biology, religious studies and needlework. I also took CSEs in the same subjects, as well as additional CSEs in art and maths.

For O levels, I was allocated a new set of teachers. My English teacher was Mrs Humphries, who hailed from Liverpool. She was the typical hippy, with long hair worn in plaits, small wire-rimmed glasses and long, floaty skirts. She was a vibrant and enthusiastic teacher who inspired in me a love of writing and storytelling.

History was taught by Mrs Duncan, who seemed to have a fixation on the Industrial Revolution, ramming home the names and dates of great inventors like Crompton, Cartwright and Hargreaves, until they almost became intimate acquaintances.

Our religious studies teacher was Mr Bradbury. He was a tall, thin, stooped figure, who wore half-moon spectacles and an expression of gentle benevolence as befitted his role as an instructor in religious and moral ethics. Many of my classmates thought he was eccentric, but I enjoyed his thought-provoking debates. Our needlework teacher was Mrs Edwards, a large, blustery, no-nonsense lady.

One of my favourite lessons was art, and that was because I liked my art teacher Mr Reynard. He was a young, 'hip' teacher with a penchant for the avant-garde who imbued in us a love of abstract designs and concepts, fixated as he was with bold colours and surreal designs. As befitted his arty temperament, he wore his hair swept back and probably a bit longer than was permissible for a teacher, and his shirts were always teamed up with a kipper tie in bold green-and-orange geometric patterns. He didn't seem like a teacher, in that he never shouted or told us off. I don't remember him ever raising his voice to us. Art opened up a whole world of imagery and fantasy for me, though sadly I lacked any real artistic ability and failed to get a coveted high-grade CSE.

I have Radio Luxembourg to thank for helping to sweeten the stodgy diet of homework and exam revision that always seemed to lie heavily on me during my fourth and fifth years at St Aidan's. Locked away in my bedroom night after night with my tiny transistor radio for company, I welcomed the Scottish burr of Stuart Henry and the smooth tones of Paul Burnett and Tony Prince as diversions to the tedium of memorising the key functions of the human endocrine system or the unique limestone formations of Malham Cove.

Radio Luxembourg was an independent commercial radio station and a popular listening choice for seventies teenagers like me. It was launched as a backlash against the British Broadcasting Corporation (later to become the BBC) claiming supremacy over broadcasting rights, and was a forerunner to a number of pirate radio stations, the most notable of these being Radio Caroline which operated from a ship moored off the coast of southern England back in the sixties.

But the highlight of the radio week, for me, was listening to Radio One's *Pick of the Pops* featuring the top twenty hit singles in the charts. This Sunday teatime ritual was presented by Alan 'Fluff' Freeman, best remembered for his catchphrase, 'Not 'arf, pop-pickers.' Oh, the excitement of finding out which song had reached the number-one slot! Would it be Alice Cooper, scarily dressed in gothic black, long hair flowing wildly, looking like a distant cousin of Heathcliff, screaming 'School's Out'? Or would it be my very own Rod Stewart crooning 'You Wear It Well'?

By then, I'd amassed quite a collection of singles and albums, all paid for through my hard-earned money from Hallett's. Many of these have survived to the present day, although they're now a bit warped and scratchy sounding. Like many teenagers, my record buying was heavily influenced by the singles charts. For example, when Chicory Tip's 'Son of My Father', with its catchy synthesised beat, skipped up the charts in 1972 I just knew I'd have to buy my own copy. Once home, I'd insist on playing it over and over again on our Dansette record player, until everyone in the house – Mum, Dad, brother, baby – had been driven insane by its inane lyrics and cheesy tune.

Another high point of the week was watching *Top of the Pops* and seeing my idols perform live in front of a studio audience. Every Thursday evening at 7.30 p.m. my mum, brother and I would settle down to watch the half-hour long *Top of the Pops* show, riveted by the young dancers in the audience in their seventies garb – flared trousers, chiffon blouses, platform shoes, uniform of every savvy teenage pop-picker – jiggling and wiggling to the likes of The Who, Mott the Hoople, Faces, et al. belting out their hit songs just a few feet away. What these young folk probably didn't realise was that they were setting the trends for me and millions of other teenagers up and down the country who aped their clothing and dance moves.

In the seventies, as with the sixties, sitting around the television was something we all did as family. There were lots of entertainment programmes that held universal appeal. Who could forget *Morecambe and Wise* with their irrepressible comedy? They brought their own unique brand of sunshine in to living rooms across the land. As a teenager I didn't always understand the mischievous undercurrent of innuendo that was Morecambe and Wise's stock-in-trade, but I loved the way they gently poked fun at their guests. Illustrious stars, such as Shirley Bassey, Peter Cushing, Sir Lawrence Olivier, André (Preview)

Previn, and Angela Rippon were among those who became the subjects of the duo's mirth.

Then, of course, there was Val Doonican. This Irish crooner, with his genteel charm and quirky trademark knitted jumpers, enthralled his legions of fans with his Saturday night entertainment show. At the end of each show, he would croon a gentle ballad as he relaxed in his rocking chair. It was the equivalent of sucking on a peppermint sweet: soothing and comforting. He always seemed to me to be a perpetually old man, though in truth he was probably only in his forties at that time. *The Val Doonican Show* became part of our Saturday night staple viewing. Granny and Grandad were among his many fans, and a collection of his LPs sat proudly in their elegant stereogram alongside the likes of Bing Crosby, Andy Williams and Lonnie Donegan.

Val Doonican and his contemporaries, with their gentle ballads, became a welcome antidote to the dark days of unrest and industrial strife which dominated the seventies. Television news and newspaper headlines were depressingly full of bad news, dominated by the miners' strikes, power cuts, the introduction of the three-day week, economic gloom, and the IRA bombings. However, it's probably fair to say these national events largely escaped my notice, wrapped up as I was in my own cotton-wool-ball world of adolescent self-absorption, a world defined by school, homework, boys, dance, fashion, and pop music, though not necessarily in that order. My world was cosseted, narcissistic, and self-centred. But I was probably no different from any other teenager, then or now.

32

'Ballroom Blitz'

The girl in the bedroom mirror gazing back at me is a round-faced, slightly pudgy fifteen-year-old, her dimpled cheeks framed by mousy, shoulder-length, wavy hair, coaxed into something approximating a seventies hairstyle – soft flicks at the fringe and sides. She is wearing the skimpiest of brown hot pants and a loose-fitting billowy green blouse with long puffed sleeves. To complete the look, a brown-and-orange chiffon scarf is artfully draped around her neck. Her face is painted with vivid green eyeshadow, thick black mascara and coral lipstick. As she scrutinises her appearance carefully in the mirror, her reverie is broken by the opening of the door.

'If you think you're going out dressed like that you've got another thing coming!' shrieks the girl's mother, marching into the room.

In the battle that ensues, there are concessions to be made: the hot pants can stay (after all, everyone is wearing them, even the girl's mum) but the make-up has to go. Or, at the very least, be toned down.

'It makes you look too old,' the girl's mum snaps, in a desperate attempt to cling to the last vestiges of her daughter's childhood and protect her from the unwelcome advances of male suitors. The mother may also, perhaps, be reflecting winsomely on her own teenage days and her own incipient middle age.

The girl was me, getting ready for my first 'grown-up' dance at Cockerham – and becoming stroppier by the minute. By this point, we'd outgrown youth club. With the demise of Stalmine disco, we were ready to look beyond the frontiers of Over Wyre for our dancing. The discovery of dances in the nearby villages of Cockerham and St Michael's opened up new opportunities for meeting people outside our own close-knit community and offered the tantalising promise of a more mature social scene.

Dances were held on Saturday nights, alternating between Cockerham and St Michael's. Both dances were long established, following a tradition that dated back to the fifties and beyond, when nearly every village hall in the district hosted its own dance where teenagers waltzed, quickstepped, foxtrotted and jived the night away.

John Higginson, a retired poultry farmer and agricultural historian from Pilling, can remember the days of those early ballroom dances with fond affection. Back then, rural young folk – many farmers and farmworkers – flocked to the nearest village hall on their bikes and motorbikes, or in their cars if they were lucky enough to afford one, to dance their way to romance. Dances were packed to the rafters and each dance would have its own resident dance band and lead singer, crooning to tunes inspired by the likes of Josef Locke, Frank Sinatra, Bing Crosby and Frankie Laine.

According to John, village dances served a vital function: they ensured the Over Wyre population flourished – for they became an unofficial courting club, a place where the delicate pink tips of romance blossomed into full-bloomed love, courtship, marriage and children. Ask him, and John has no hesitation in rattling off the names of husbands and wives who first clapped eyes on each other in a dusty village hall, and who are still living in matrimonial harmony more than fifty years later, having made their own contribution to population growth by propagating a generation of Over Wyre offspring.

Back in his dancing days, it was local band the Silver Keynotes who kept their young audiences in the mood for dancing. The Keynotes were versatile enough to play a selection of melodies to capture the mood of a quickstep, a waltz, a foxtrot or a barn dance, later adding rock 'n' roll to their repertoire.

The band consisted of brothers Arthur and John Huntington, on saxophone and accordion respectively, saxophonist Geoff Angel, accordionist John Wilding, guitarist and vocalist Bill Sutcliffe, drummer Melvyn Bilsborough and guitarist Colin Davis. They were farmers, motor mechanics and joiners by day, and debonair band musicians by night, dressed in specially tailored suits as they graced the stage singing the melodies of Neil Sedaka, Pat Boone and Elvis Presley.

The Silver Keynotes were known throughout the district, becoming a regular fixture at weekly dances in the villages of Claughton, St Michael's, Winmarleigh and Chipping, as well as travelling further afield to North Yorkshire, performing six nights a week. Later, two of their members, Melvyn Bilsborough and Colin Davies – together with Melvyn Stafford – formed their own three-piece harmony band, the Sleepwalkers. They became known as the district's answer to The Bachelors, performing in clubs across the north west.

All of this was before my time, of course. But John Higginson remembers the era with fondness. There was a strict dress code: smart suits and shirt and tie for men, elegant cotton dresses for the ladies. John recalled having his own bespoke suit made by St Michael's-based tailor, Arthur Fisher. It lasted for years.

Dances were lively events but if anyone was caught trying to pick a fight they would have burly Silver Keynotes singer 'Big' Bill Sutcliffe to deal with. At the first hint of trouble, Bill would hurl himself off the stage and frogmarch the offenders out of the dance hall before they could so much as utter 'Moon River.' Unruffled, Bill would then straighten his cuffs, step back on stage and carry on playing as if nothing had happened.

Midway through the dance, supper was served. John

remembers paying one shilling and sixpence for two sandwiches, a packet of crisps, a cake and a cup of tea – no booze – served by Nellie Kirkby, who led the team of dance-hall caterers.

It was a decade or so later before I followed John's dancing footsteps to the Cockerham and St Michael's dances. By 1972, Cockerham dance had an entirely different feel: for a start, the dancing was less genteel, the gentle waltz and quickstep having been sidestepped by the new frenetic beat of disco. Dancing was less about couples and more about individual self-expression: you didn't need a partner; you didn't have to sit around like a wallflower waiting for someone to invite you on to the dance floor; you could get out there and do your own thing, wiggling your hips, waving your arms and moving your feet to the disco beat. And the dress code was anything but formal, reflecting the eclectic tastes of seventies fashion.

Both Cockerham and St Michael's were well-organised dances, and for the princely sum of thirty pence upon admission, we could have a really good night out. As you paid to enter, your hand was date-stamped so that you could go out and return later without having to pay again (though going outside was still a definite no-no as far as my parents were concerned). As with Stalmine disco, there were still fights but these were usually swiftly broken up by the burly bouncers, beefy farmworkers and amateur wrestlers by day, who doubled up as godfathers of the dance hall by night.

As in John Higginson's day, the Silver Keynotes were still the resident dance band, although by my time the band's line-up had changed, many of the original members having left to be replaced by newer musicians. Sadly, despite my best efforts, I have been unable to track down any of the Keynotes who were playing during my dancing days, which is a pity really because it would have been nice to share some reminiscences. But what I do remember is their repertoire of seventies melodies including 'Knock Three Times on the Ceiling' by Dawn, along with a spirited version of 'Mony Mony' by Tommy James and the Shondells. And they always closed the night with a slow smoochie last-waltz number.

In between the band playing, a DJ spun the latest records. By 1972, glam rock was making its own spangly mark on music and fashion, with artistes like Gary Glitter, David Bowie, T. Rex, Sweet, Roxy Music and Slade setting the bar for ostentation. With their new zany over-the-top outfits, in gold lamé, silver latex, sequins and glitter, each tried to outdo the other in their shows of flamboyance and attitude. Bowie was the first of a line of pop stars to trend androgyny, his spiky hair, dramatic clown-like eye make-up and gender-neutral clothes denoting that curious fusion of masculine/feminine, man/woman.

I loved T. Rex, and in particular their charismatic lead singer Mark Bolan, the archetypal pretty boy with his black curly hair, winsome kohl-rimmed eyes and effete pout. Needless to say, their early records, 'Jeepster', 'Ride A White Swan' and 'Hot Love' were swiftly added to my collection of 45 rpm vinyls. I embraced glam-rock fashion, buying myself a loose-fitting glittery top in silver lurex that twinkled and sparkled. I can remember teaming this with plain black trousers, and feeling like I'd reached the zenith of glam-rock couture, though in truth I probably looked more like an animated Christmas tree.

Cockerham and St Michael's were also the meeting place for local rock 'n' roll aficionados. During the seventies, rock 'n' roll made a revival (some might argue it never went away), segueing neatly into the glam-rock era to create a colourful carnival of style and youthful exuberance. A gang of rock 'n' rollers from Garstang dominated the dance floor, jiving and throwing themselves backwards and forwards to the beat of Eddie Cochrane's 'Summertime Blues', Jerry Lee Lewis's 'Great Balls of Fire', and the Electric Light Orchestra's 'Roll Over Beethoven' with a full fury of athleticism and style.

Wearing leather jackets, drainpipe trousers and winkle-pickers, their hair deliciously slicked back, these guys were every inch solid gold rock 'n' roll, and eminently fanciable – think John Travolta and *Grease*, and you have the picture. They were led by brothers, Mick and John Piela, from Garstang. It's perhaps no surprise that Mick, having started his teens going to local youth clubs and dance halls, later developed a professional career as a youth worker, eventually becoming district manager of the Wyre Youth Service.

Getting ready to go to a dance required hours, if not days, of preparation. I can remember us counting the days to the next dance from Mondays onwards; by Friday afternoons we were almost ecstatic with anticipation. During the week, we'd plan what we were going to wear. Each Saturday afternoon, we'd congregate in someone's bedroom in order to wash and do up our hair. Where we met would depend on whose parents' turn it was to drive us to our dance. So if it was my dad's turn to drive, we would meet in my bedroom; if it was Lynn's dad's turn, we would meet at her house, three or four of us giggling and chatting inanely, as we helped each other out with our Carmen rollers.

Hairstyles were generally feminine, with long feather cuts and big flicks to the side. They may have looked soft and natural, but this often belied hours of painstaking work with rollers to coax your locks into looking like Clodagh Rodgers, the glamorous Irish singer who entered the Eurovision Song Contest with her catchy 'Jack in the Box' in 1971. Boys' hairstyles were also quite long, in comparison to today. They were typically collar length with a thick floppy fringe, teamed with long sideburns – or sideys as they were known then. But if you were a boy and into heavy rock music, following the likes of Deep Purple and Black Sabbath, then you might opt to grow your hair long and wild.

Back then, it was fashionable for girls to pluck their eyebrows. It was an eye-wateringly painful act of self-destruction that quite literally brought tears to your eyes. You'd take a pair of tweezers and pluck out each hair mercilessly, one by one, until you were left with a pencil-thin line of brow hair. You'd then apply a coat of Vaseline across each reddened brow and then carefully and methodically apply eyebrow pencil in order to create a new pair of artificially defined eyebrows. My once thick, bushy eyebrows all but disappeared as a consequence of my overzealous plucking. To this day, I remain virtually eyebrowless, having brutally plucked them all away in homage to the seventies craze for pencil-thin eyebrows.

Make-up consisted of powdered eyeshadow in a spectrum of blues and greens and turquoise. Back then, it was fashionable to apply pearlised eye cream, in luminous white, in the space between the eyelids and eyebrows. The purpose of this was to accentuate the eyes but in reality it probably gave a whole new meaning to 'glow in the dark', making us look like a cross between a glow-worm and a bit part player from an extra-terrestrial movie. Lashings of Boots Seventeen mascara, a dab of blusher and a dash of budget-price pearlised lipstick from Rimmel, a liberal smear of Clearasil to clear any wayward spots and we were all dolled up and good to go.

Despite my mum's protestations, I manage to defy her 'only a little make-up' rule by smuggling my make-up purse to the dance in my handbag; once I reached the dance hall, I'd make a beeline for the toilets and apply lashings of eyeshadow and lipstick to a face already flushed by adrenalin and anticipation. Although I never realised it at the time, in my act of subterfuge I was following a family template set in place by two of my ancestors, half a century or so earlier.

Florrie and Dorothy were two of my grandma's sisters. They were the daughters of my great-grandma, Irish-born Dorothy Ward, by all accounts a tyrant who forbade her teenage daughters from going to dances. Apparently Florrie and Dorothy, so our family story goes, used to resort to lies and subterfuge. They would tell her they were going to church, when in reality they were attending an evening dance in their home town of Padiham, near Burnley. Dressed up in their church clothes, they would sneak out to their dance venue and change into their finery before dancing started. Later, the whole process would be repeated in reverse, and they would meekly creep home in their church attire, with Grandma Ward none the wiser about their escapades. Having heard this story, it's clear that in my little act of make-up deception I had inherited some of Florrie and Dorothy's traits!

When I first asked my parents if I could go to Cockerham and St Michael's, it was with those same three conditions that had marked their grudging approval to me attending Preesall youth club and Stalmine disco – one: be ready when we come to pick you up; two: no smoking; and three: no 'going outside.' But by now I was a couple of years older.

At fifteen, going on sixteen, I was ready to cross that great parental border control checkpoint and venture into the uncharted territory of teenage experimentation.

Like many teenagers, then and now, my first experiment was with alcohol. It happened when I was with friends, and we were dropped off at St Michael's village hall for a Saturday night dance. No sooner had we piled out of the parental car and watched as it zoomed away into the night, than we did a U-turn, confidently marching down the road to The Grapes pub.

There were nearly always some older lads hanging round outside, cigarette in one hand, pint of lager in the other, and we managed to persuade some of them to buy us a vodka and lime. I'll never forget sloping inside the pub, and that intoxicating thrill of doing something illicit and bold, mingled with fear of getting caught and found out. So you can imagine how I felt when the local bobby walked in, just as I'd downed the last of my drink.

Casting his magisterial eye around the crowded bar area, he

looked at the line-up of empty glasses. Then at the sea of anxious faces.

'Take this as a warning, all of you,' he pronounced sombrely. 'If I catch any of you here again, I'll be contacting your parents, one by one. Now, out you go. And don't let me see you again!'

My parents never did find out about this. It's just as well they didn't, because that would have brought a swift and ignominious end to my dance-hall days.

Experiment number two occurred at Cockerham dance, and this time it was with cigarettes. I'd befriended a Scottish boy who was staying with his auntie in Pilling. I think his name was Eddie. He was about the same age as me, and a regular smoker. He asked me if I'd like a puff of his cigarette. Naturally, this was in the days before smoking was banned in public places so it was permissible to smoke at dances, which meant you had to wade through a nicotine-shrouded fog each time you stepped on the dance floor. I can remember taking a puff of his Players No. 6 and nearly choking after inhaling the rich, noxious substance. It took two or three more cigarettes before I could cultivate a look of cool nonchalance, dancing to Bowie's 'Gene Genie', cigarette in hand, a brazen accessory in an era of 'glamboyance.'

In truth, I never really latched on to cigarettes, short of that experimentation with their toxic charms at Cockerham village hall and a later brief flirtation with Consulate cool menthol flavoured cigarettes soon after leaving school. But even the minty taste of Consulate could not disguise what, to me, felt like ingesting the equivalent of toilet cleaner. This, of course, with the insight gained from subsequent years of working in health promotion, is exactly what it was, ammonia being one of several hundred noxious substances contained in cigarettes.

Thanks to the sage advice of Cathy and Claire in *Jackie*, coupled with non-stop nagging from our parents, it was easier to resist being lured into sexual experimentation, despite the era of the pill and its allure of permissiveness. Some boys were brash, or uncouth, enough to go around brandishing 'rubber johnnies' in search of someone willing to forsake their reputation for a night of illicit copulation. But most girls clung to the bible of good sense advocated by the two agony aunts and abstained from doing anything that could jeopardise their reputation or their entire future. And it's fair to say as a result of this there were very few, if any, schoolgirl pregnancies that I can remember, certainly not in our safe, cosy rural world.

33

'School's Out!'

We fifth formers at St Aidan's were treated differently from our younger peers. This wasn't just a nod to our growing maturity, but because we'd made a choice to stay on at school. We didn't *have* to be there. We were the last of a generation to have the option of leaving school at fifteen before ROSLA (raising of the school leaving age) came in to effect in 1973. Which meant we were offered a range of inducements to make staying on at school just that little bit more appealing.

First of all, a special building was created to house us. This was the ROSLA building, or the Lancaster Wing as it was more commonly known in school. It comprised classrooms for vocational learning: a typing room specially equipped for teaching audio-typing, a needlework room, cookery classroom, car maintenance workshop and, curiously, a flat with a self-contained kitchen. The latter was equipped with a washing machine, cooker, fridge, dining table and chairs, and an ironing board. The idea was that a small cohort of us would take time out from lessons to spend in the flat learning homemaking skills in readiness for our future roles as housewives.

I can't remember any of the boys having to undertake these duties, but certainly we girls did, and we relished the opportunity to skive from lessons for a week or so, under the pretext of cooking, washing and ironing. As one of our assigned tasks we were required to plan, budget for, and prepare a meal for our teachers. I have no recollection of what my cohort chose to dish up, but I would imagine it would have been something along the lines of toad-in-the-hole with watery vegetables, followed by steamed pudding, staples of the seventies diet. We were two decades removed from notions of the fifties housewife, but attitudes died hard, even in this era of so-called female enlightenment. Ah, the joys of discovering what lay ahead of us after school!

As another concession to our growing maturity, we fifth-formers had our own uniform, distinct from that of younger pupils. Each year, the upcoming fifth-form girls were given a choice of what to wear. It felt like an enormous privilege. In our uniform planning sessions with needlework teacher Mrs Edwards we had long discussions on what we would wear, and it seemed to take ages to reach a consensus. In the end, we opted for dresses in purple polyester with a patterned bodice and decorative feature buttons and billowy long sleeves, gathered and buttoned at the cuff. There was no stipulation on length, and some dresses – my own included – were ludicrously short. We felt we were blazing a trail for seventies trend! The boys were more conservative, in black blazers or jumpers and trousers teamed with white shirts and grey ties.

There were other privileges, and one of them was being allowed to stay in the ROSLA block at lunchtime, instead of going into the playground with the rest of the school plebs. A table-tennis table was set up, and you could sit and eat your sandwiches cafeteria-style in the classroom. It was all designed to make us feel more grown-up.

During lunch breaks, a few of us would sneak in to the typing room, where a record player used during audio-typing classes lurked in the corner. Miss Borthwick, as well as being an English teacher, also taught typing. We'd put on records and practise our dance moves ready for the next Cockerham or St Michael's dance. I can remember us playing Chris Montez's catchy 'Let's

Dance' over and over, dancing in the space between the desks, using the typing room as a makeshift dance hall. Bizarrely, this wasn't even a seventies song, having made the charts in the sixties. But it had gained a resurgence in popularity among the Garstang rock 'n' rollers who populated the dance halls, and we were determined to impress them.

Strictly speaking, we weren't allowed in the typing room and we certainly weren't allowed to use the record player. One of us would always keep a watchful eye on the door in case a passing teacher heard us. There was one occasion when we were caught unguarded and one of our teachers burst in. I can't remember which one it was, but I can recall someone hastily yanking the stylus off the record player and stopping Chris Montez mid flow, while we all sat down crimson-faced, feeling like shoplifters caught in the act of stealing a tin of pilchards.

'Don't let me catch you doing this again, or I'll report you to the head,' thundered the teacher, while we sat there meekly. It didn't deter us, though we did change our tune. Next, it was T. Rex and 'Hot Love' – and stronger reinforcements at the door.

It was during the fifth year that some of my classmates started 'going steady.' Romances were born in the ROSLA wing that flourished into long-term relationships and eventual marriage. Mark Lawson and Debbie Rowe got together in the classroom, as did Ian Brook and Katrine McPhee. Both couples are still going strong to this day, both living and working locally. As for that shy, blond-haired boy from Manchester who started Pilling School on the same day as me, and who shared lessons with me at St Aidan's, well, he was too busy playing football to take any serious interest in girls, though he quietly attracted the attentions of a few. But I wasn't among them; my sights were set firmly on those Garstang rock 'n' rollers with their dark, swarthy good looks.

In 1973, the UK became a member of the EEC (European Economic Community). It was also an important year for me, with GCE O levels and CSE exams looming. Much of the fifth form was spent in a frenzy of activity, preparing for the exams that we would be taking that summer, and that would pave our entire future. There were mock exams after Christmas and in no time at all the real thing descended on us.

Coursework didn't count towards the final marks in your GCEs so everything hinged on the final exam. I can remember spending every evening closeted in my bedroom, revising feverishly while listening to Stuart Henry et al. on Radio Luxembourg.

Exams flew by and in no time at all we were leaving school. I can remember the mixed emotions on walking out of the school gates on the afternoon of my final exam – I think it was geography – one hot sunny day towards the end of June. There was the euphoria of knowing my exams were over and I was no longer a slave to petty school rules. But it also felt very strange to be leaving somewhere that had played such a big part in my life. In the glum days that followed, I felt like I'd been wrenched away from something that felt as cosy and safe and familiar to me as a pair of snug pyjamas. I can remember feeling sad and lost, and somehow dejected, an enjoyable phase of my life having vanished. I left a piece of my heart at St Aidan's that day in 1973.

School organised a school-leavers' gathering in the Lancaster Wing some time towards the end of the summer term, but I don't remember much about it. It was a low-key affair, certainly nothing like today's proms where school-leavers celebrate the end of their school career with all the razzmatazz and kitsch of a Hollywood Oscars ceremony.

Before taking my GCEs, I'd already decided to resist my parents' and teachers' ambitions for me to train as a teacher. It wasn't an overnight decision, more of a gradual creeping realisation that teaching wasn't for me, triggered by a combination of factors. I feared staying on at St Aidan's to take A levels, thinking it would be a lonely life with all my friends having deserted me to start work. Nor did I want to join any of the neighbouring schools that were better equipped to teach A levels and offered a wider range of subjects than the desultory options that would have been open to me at St Aidan's: domestic science and religious studies.

No: I wanted to go out to work, just as all my friends were doing. They were scooping glamorous-sounding jobs in secretarial work, hairdressing, jewellery shops and banks. The boys I'd been at school with were starting apprenticeships in electrical work, motor mechanics, plumbing, and joinery. A golden feast of apprenticeships was on offer, ripe for the taking. Some of my schoolmates settled in to jobs within their family businesses, working on farms or in horticulture. Even *Jackie* magazine conspired to make going out to work sound a much more attractive proposition than school, devoting articles to how to get a head start in a secretarial career.

And I'd already been given a tantalising glimpse of what the working world looked like, thanks to one of my friends, Enid Cross. Enid was one of the few girls in our year who had resisted ROSLA and decided to leave school at fifteen, getting a job at Knott End Co-op. During lunch breaks, we'd sometimes venture out of the school gates – it was another of our privileges as fifth-formers – and eat pie and chips, from the village chippy, on a bench. Enid would meet us on her half-day off, on a Wednesday. There she'd be in her green nylon overall, looking all grown-up and cheery, with money in her purse that she'd earned serving customers and organising food displays. I wanted a taste of that life. I no longer wanted to be shackled by petty school rules and more exams.

It was a decision I was to regret profoundly many years later. Looking at how today's generation are encouraged to stay on at school for their A levels and then go on to university or college, it seems almost astonishing to consider it was the norm for secondary modern kids like me to leave school at sixteen and find a job. But jobs in shops, factories and offices were in abundance and you could virtually take your pick.

I think one of the real tragedies of my generation of secondary modern pupils is that our horizons were limited by lowered expectations; school, teachers, parents and wider society seemed to expect less of us, career wise, than of our grammar school cousins. This, and the fact that work was plentiful, meant there was less of an incentive to aim higher. As far as I am aware, only one person from my school year went to university straight after school. Though I was fortunate in that I was given opportunities to progress, I rebelled because I didn't want to be different from my friends. It was a form of self-imposed pressure.

Ironically, for grammar school pupils, the reverse was true. Girls of my age who went to Fleetwood Grammar School have described to me how they were under pressure to follow an academic path, with A levels and university seen as the gateway to professional work. Those who rebelled, leaving school at sixteen in order to find a job, risked being labelled as underachievers.

Looking back, it seems a travesty to think that one exam – the eleven-plus – could be so divisive. Its tentacles reached far out into adult life, stifling aspiration among those secondary modern kids who might have gone on to achieve greater academic success. And it placed undue pressure on those from the grammar schools who were coerced in to thinking A levels and beyond were the only way to achieve a gilded future. All of this on the basis of one singular exam lasing two hours or less!

Reflecting on my decision to leave school at sixteen, I can see how very different I was from my grandma. She would have given her eye teeth to have stayed on and furthered her education but was forced by her mother, my great-grandma, to work in the mill. Alas, she was of a different generation, stifled by poverty and deprived of life chances. And yet here I was squandering this golden opportunity to 'make something of myself' because I didn't want to be any different from my friends.

My mum insisted that if I didn't want to go in to teaching, then I must look for a job 'with prospects.' The civil service seemed to fit the bill, as far as she was concerned, offering the golden corridor to a steady career with 'good promotion prospects and a pension.' But the application process for civil service jobs was long and tortuous. I was impatient, and I wanted work immediately. After leaving school that summer, I decided to apply for secretarial jobs while awaiting the outcome of my civil service application.

Mum and I trudged around Blackpool, with me attending interview after interview, prim in my suit of pink polyester. I went for a job as a clerical assistant at Carley's Continental Fashions, in Birley, thinking how glamorous it would be to work in one of Blackpool's top fashion shops. 'Too quiet and shy,' was the response.

Another interview followed at a solicitor's office. 'Lacks typing experience,' they told me afterwards.

A job as a library assistant at *The Evening Gazette*, filing news cuttings, looked promising. 'Yes, we like you,' said the glamorous blonde lady who interviewed me. 'But we feel it's going to be too far for you to travel from Pilling.' It was very solicitous of her to think of me, but it didn't get me the job.

Eventually, a letter plopped through the door. It was an invitation to go for an interview as an administrative assistant in the civil service. I can't remember much about my interview but I must have said the right things because a few weeks later I received a letter to say I'd got the job on the condition that I passed three GCE O levels, one of which had to be English.

The summer of 1973 was one of nervous anticipation. On the day of my GCE results, one gloomy August afternoon, I'd gone to Blackpool Pleasure Beach with some friends. I can remember phoning my mum from a public call box to see how I'd gone on.

She must have phoned the school to find out my results – why I hadn't done this myself, I'm not sure.

'You've got five passes and one fail,' she relayed, before adding that the school hadn't told her which subjects I'd passed and which one I'd failed. My heart sank, and a feeling of sickness washed over me. What if it was English I'd failed? I visualised my secure career as a civil servant vanishing before my eyes.

Calling in to school the following day, I made the joyous discovery that I'd passed my English language O level with a respectable grade two. I'd gained grade three for both history and human biology and I'd passed geography and religious studies at grade six. I was proudly in possession of a clutch of five GCE O levels – more than enough to get me through the doors of the civil service. My one failure was in needlework and dressmaking. Was I concerned about that? Was I fiddlesticks! I was nearly seventeen, about to make my first heady steps in to the world of work, and housewifely pursuits couldn't have been further from my mind.

But any dreams of a golden career climbing through the echelons of the civil service quickly subsided when I first walked in to the fortress of bureaucracy. The heavily guarded site was a labyrinth of corridors and office blocks, all identical in their bleakness and smelling of the ink of officialdom. I often wondered whether the security guards were there to prevent staff from escaping, rather than preventing criminals from entering.

Before starting, I'd had visions of bright conversations with interesting colleagues as we swiftly worked our way through mountains of stimulating papers and dealt with telephone enquiries from the grateful public. I thought I'd be inspired, motivated, energised by my role as a tiny but vital cog in this vast powerhouse. I couldn't have been more wrong.

As an administrative assistant, I was responsible for checking buff-coloured records to make sure names and dates tallied. The work was dreary, monotonous and sporadic, with yawning gaps in activity, the only thing to look forward to being the welcoming rattle of the tea trolley laden with cakes, pushed by a cheery lady in white overalls, at about eleven o'clock.

My colleagues were old, or so they appeared to me, fresh-faced and brimming with vitality at sixteen. Among them was a leering bachelor of about fifty who kept making lascivious comments about my legs. There was a grumpy chap, Carl, a shirker, his flaccid features bearing the hallmarks of someone who has been ground down by years of institutionalisation, sunken and drained of lifeblood. There was a crotchety spinster who remained stuck like glue to her chair in a corner, nose buried in papers, refusing to engage in conversation. I think she only discovered she had legs when the bell sounded for the 4.30 p.m. finish. And there was Jenny, a cigarette-smoking former factory boss, who greedily grasped piles of files when they arrived and worked through them at breakneck speed as if to a life-or-death deadline. And then crumpled and sighed with boredom when it was all finished.

After six months, I could feel myself slipping into a slough of depression and despondency. The days dragged and I feared becoming another Carl, trapped within greying walls and endless corridors, until I was dusty, white and old, bleached of energy, drowning in ennui. Perhaps I was unfortunate in the office I'd been assigned to. I knew of other girls who'd started at the same time as me and they were busily engaged in their work, enjoying every minute. But I knew the civil service wasn't for me, a young woman on the precipice of adulthood seeking a stimulating career. I had to find a way of escaping.

The chance to flee came when I spotted an advertisement in my local paper, *The Garstang Courier*. It was for a junior reporter. Just the sort of thing I'd been looking for! They wanted someone with five GCEs, including English, and who enjoyed writing and meeting people and was interested in local affairs. I knew I could tick all these boxes!

I wrote a letter outlining how I had always longed to pursue a career in journalism (despite what Mr Gledhill had told me in my careers interview), adding that I was in possession of five good GCE passes, that I loved writing and enjoyed meeting people and that I knew quite a lot about local goings-on. I think I may have mentioned in the letter that my step-grandad, Bill Allen, was Mayor of Preesall, and that I knew something about local councils and how they worked (I didn't, but I knew it would only take half an hour or so with Grandad Bill to get myself acquainted).

It must have pressed the right buttons because within a matter of days a letter arrived from the editor, Tom Dooley, inviting me for an interview. For some unfathomable reason that is probably best only understood by those who are in their teens and have a casual attitude to things like time management, on the morning of the interview I went shopping to Blackpool on the number 85 bus with my friend, Vivien. That day, I can distinctly remember buying Tina Turner's catchy disco song, 'Nutbush (City Limits)' from a record shop. I gave it to Vivien to look after because I needed to catch a different bus – the 142 from Blackpool to Morecambe via Garstang – in order to attend my interview later that day, and I didn't want to be saddled with shopping.

The office of *The Courier* was a shabby little place above the stairs of a stationery shop in Garstang's Church Street. During the interview, Tom – runner-bean tall, stooped, bespectacled with straggly tufts of red hair pulled across his forehead and a gruff Yorkshire accent – puffed on his cigar as he asked me about my schoolwork, my writing and what motivated me to apply for the post of junior reporter.

'So, Angela,' he commenced. 'What made you decide to apply for this job?'

'Well, I enjoy writing and I think I'm quite good at writing stories,' I responded tentatively.

'And?' he prompted.

'And I'm interested in local news,' I added, hopefully.

'Tell me what you know about local news.'

'Well, I know there's a lot going on with the councils ...'

'Yes?' he prompted.

'I know that councils have changed, and that Preesall Council has had to make way for Wyre Borough Council and a lot of councillors aren't happy about that because they think they will lose a lot of their power,' I stuttered, keen to show my newly acquired knowledge of the 1974 Local Government Act, gleaned from talking to Grandad Bill.

'What powers do they have?'

'They talk about things like dog dirt and look at planning applications.'

I told him I liked writing poetry, which was a slight deviation from the truth as I'd never written much, short of a few lines of scribble, but I saw the bright light bulb of interest register in his eyes. After what seemed like hours, Tom thanked me for my time and said he would be in touch. I went home, feeling exhausted, convinced that I'd let the job of my dreams slip through my grasp.

A few days later I received a letter from Tom. He wrote that he was concerned because I didn't drive. He wondered how I'd get to work, if I was offered the job. With a groan of despair, I could see invisible slippery hands wrenching any hope of this job away from me. I wrote back straight away to say I'd be able to catch a bus from Pilling to Garstang each day, and that once I reached seventeen I would be learning to drive and hoped to pass my test.

I never did get my Tina Turner record back from Vivien, but I did get the job! I was ecstatic when a letter arrived congratulating me on a successful interview and offering me a role as a junior reporter. This was my chance of a dream career, a chance to carve out a thrilling future, to see my name in print, to be 'someone'. Tom told me afterwards that his letter had been a little test to see how keen I was. My swift letter in reply had been enough to convince him that I was hungry for the job.

My parents shared my jubilation. They'd seen how unhappy I'd been at the civil service and were relieved that I'd found a job that would offer me more in the way of satisfaction, variety and stimulation than my civil service position, even though they knew journalism was highly competitive field, fraught with insecurities, and poorly paid in comparison with many careers. My mum, I think, secretly harboured notions of me being the next Marjorie Proops, or Jean Rook, in those days a columnist on the *Daily Express*.

'Angela's been offered a job on *The Garstang Courier*. She's going to be a journalist,' she'd proudly tell everyone she met – family, friends, neighbours – much to my embarrassment. There may well have been a touch of envy in her proclamation. Like her mother, my grandma, she was literary-minded and enjoyed reading, and later in life she went to creative writing classes. It's perhaps a tragic irony of her choice to remain a stay-at-home mum that she felt compelled to live her life vicariously through her children, never really finding her own niche until it was too late, by which time her deteriorating health had stifled any opportunities she might have had to make something of herself.

I resigned from the civil service and started my job as a junior reporter on *The Garstang Courier* on 4 May 1974. It was the beginning of an exciting new chapter in my life. I was seventeen and a half years old, a raw talent about to unleash myself on the heady world of print journalism.

34

Extra, Extra! Read All About It!

I can recall the first day of my job at *The Courier* as if it were yesterday. It was a pale spring day, a Wednesday, and it was memorable for three reasons: firstly, I had a wrestling match with a monster of a typewriter as I tried – and failed – dozens of times to write my first ever story, a cricket report two paragraphs long. Secondly, I was taken to the local pub at lunchtime to mark my initiation as *The Courier*'s new junior reporter. And thirdly, my boss sent me home mid-afternoon, causing my mother a great deal of consternation. On top of all that, I met my new work colleagues, a lively, if unorthodox, bunch of characters.

That morning at home, tummy jittering, I dress in a sensible brown skirt and beige cardigan. In my matching brown leather handbag, at my mum's behest, I carry a blue spiral-bound reporter's notebook and blue biro – the tools of my trade. My heart beating with anticipation, I walk to the bus stop to await the Ribble Knott End to Garstang bus. When it arrives, it's full of primary school kids. Their incessant shouting ignites a firework of irritation inside my head.

On the short walk from Garstang bus station to *The Courier* office in Church Street, just off Garstang's busy High Street, I take each step tentatively. Opening the door to the little stationery shop, I'm greeted by the friendly face of Marian, the manager, a tall, smartly dressed middle-aged lady, wearing a navy bow-fronted blouse, her hair in immaculate brown curls.

'I'm the new junior reporter,' I tell her, keen to emphasise the 'junior' bit.

'Ah, you must be Angela. Welcome to our happy home,' she chuckles warmly, her tones betraying more than a hint of irony. 'Let me take you upstairs.'

I follow her up the creaky steps and along the olive-green lino-floored corridor to Tom Dooley's airy front office. All around me I can hear typewriters clattering, people chattering, the telephone ringing with shrill persistence. Here I am, in the nerve centre of a busy rural newspaper. I can smell the frenzy.

Tom shows me my office. It's a small windowless room, probably not much more than five feet squared, with a glass panel in the roof allowing just a little of the watery sunlight to peek through. In the centre is a wooden desk, topped with the biggest typewriter I've ever seen – a menacing looking Olivetti in bottle green, with an imposing set of keys; it sits there imperiously, seeming to be eyeing me gamely. Beneath the desk is a strategically placed grey metal wastepaper bin. Little do I realise how much this will get used in the coming hours, days and months.

'Right,' Tom tells me. 'Your first job is to type out a cricket report for me.' He hands over two pages of neat handwritten prose describing, down to the last wicket, Garstang first eleven's cricketing triumph the previous weekend, sent in by one of the paper's many correspondents. 'I want you to summarise this in no more than three short paragraphs.'

The Olivetti seems to be defying me, knowingly. I have never used a typewriter before. At school, I shunned Miss Borthwick's typing classes in favour of art. Now, I feel I'm about to go in to battle, knowing my incompetence will be laid bare.

'Don't worry, it's something we've all had to learn,' says Tom, as if reading my thoughts. 'You'll be surprised how quickly you get the hang of it.'

Back then, journalists wrote their 'copy' on thin strips of

paper. They remind me of the hard, scratchy toilet paper we had back in primary school. Tom shows me how to feed the copy paper into the typewriter. Following his instructions, I insert two strips of copy paper, separated by a sheet of carbon paper, in to the 'mouth' of the Olivetti and turn the handle at the side to guide the paper in, so that it can rest snugly inside. Tom leaves me to get on with the task as I stare at the pristine piece of paper in front of me – and the Olivetti glares back at me with its steely eyes in cold defiance.

I start jabbing at the keys with my two index fingers, and line of random letters spills out across the page. It looks like something out of a foreign language book and reads like gobbledygook. Hot tears of fury pricking my eyes, I yank the paper out of the machine and hurl it in the bin. I try again … and yet again … but each time I can only manage to create an incoherent jumble of letters. The Olivetti is voracious, gobbling up copy paper. Two hours and a wastepaper basket full of discarded paper later, I manage to produce a scanty two-sentence cricket report that reads something like this:

Garstang cricket's first team beat Chorley by forty-seven runs.
There was a strong performance by the batsman Tony Martin.

Tom takes my first piece of 'copy' from me and tactfully suggests that I might want to start practising my typing skills. To soothe my shattered nerves he proposes we have coffee, showing me the 'kitchen.' I'm horrified to discover that the kettle, brewing utensils and sink are housed in the same room as the ladies' loo, which would no doubt rank as a health and safety officer's nightmare these days! Over an undecidedly dodgy cup of coffee, Tom tells me a bit about *The Courier*.

The paper is part of Lancaster and Morecambe Newspapers, a small company which operates a parent paper, *The Morecambe Visitor*, and another sister paper, *The Longridge News*. The

Courier is printed from the Morecambe office. As I listen intently, he describes how *The Courier*'s circulation area covers Garstang and the surrounding villages, a wide geographical area stretching from Knott End and the coast in the west to the remoter villages of Bleasdale and Whitechapel to the east. The hub of activity is in Garstang itself, a small market town with a historic cross, a castle – Greenhalgh Castle – besieged by Cromwell's army between 1644 and 1645, and a thriving little shopping centre that serves as the nucleus for the local village and farming community.

'For a small paper, we do very well,' Tom tells me. 'But you won't find a lot of 'hard' news around here, the sort of stuff that fills the nationals and dailies – crime, disasters, major incidents, that sort of thing. So here we rely on human-interest stories – stories about people. And that's where you come in. I want you to go out there and find them.'

I learn how golden weddings, retirements, people's triumphs and tragedies and unusual hobbies are all part of the lifeblood of a local weekly paper. I discover that the Women's Institute, the parish council, the agricultural show committee, schools, churches and shops are our main fodder for news.

'Stories about people are what fill a paper like *The Courier*.' Tom warms to his theme. 'And for every person you meet, there will be a story there somewhere.'

Introduced to my new work colleagues, I quickly form the impression there will never be a dull moment in this job, for they seem a motley crew. Sharing the office with Tom is his son, Jack, who is a couple of years older than me and the paper's chief reporter; in fact, until now, he's been the only reporter on the small editorial team. Jack is tall, slim, shy-looking and he strikes me as being a bit nervy. Moody Jack, I soon discover, rarely smiles, but when he does his face lights up with a perfect set of dazzling molars.

The photographer, Johnny Smart, is beavering away in his

darkroom, where there is a strong chemical smell of photos being processed. He wipes his hands on a towel and greets me cautiously, with a mumbled 'hello.' Johnny is stocky, flatulent, dark-haired with thick black glasses and, like many in the newspaper business as I later find out, hides his sensitive side under a veneer of bluster and aloofness.

On the advertising team, there's Bob, the advertisement manager, sharp-suited, debonair and handsome with thick slate-grey hair and a wide toothy smile, with a prominent front gold filling. He reeks of aftershave and forced bonhomie. There's Dolly – a Tammy Wynette lookalike, with long flowing blonde hair and eyes that fizzle and crack with mischief and mirth under her false eyelashes. As a display advertisement rep, it's her job sell to display advertisement space to shops and businesses. With her infectious personality, it's easy to imagine Dolly selling ice cream to Eskimos. I soon discover this is an office where humour and banter are part of the job description, and flirty Dolly is at the heart of all this.

But it's Nigel Jones, the motors rep, responsible for selling advertisement space to car dealers, I warm to the most. Cigar-smoking Nigel is a little sparrow of a man with a prominent nose, pointy chin, florid cheeks, laughing eyes and an infectious chuckle that resounds throughout the office. He greets me genially, shaking my hand, cackling broadly and spluttering on his cigar as he speaks.

'Welcome to our crazy little team, Angela,' he says, grinning. 'You'll soon get used to us, but don't be surprised if we lead you astray from time to time.' Seeing my puzzled look, he tells me this means adjourning to the pub, an obligatory part of any self-respecting newspaper's routine back then, as I'm about to discover.

Finally, there's Jean, a sullen girl with long blonde hair, of a similar age to me, who is responsible for taking calls from the busy switchboard and dealing with classified advertisements

– births, marriages and deaths, cats and budgies for sale, and other smaller adverts. In the shop downstairs, Marian, the shop manager, and her assistant, Janet, also take classified adverts as well as selling an assortment of cards and stationery products.

At twelve o'clock, Tom pops his head around the door of my office, where I've been given the task of familiarising myself with back copies of *The Courier*.

'Because this is your first day here, I'm going to buy you a drink in the pub. We're going to celebrate.' Seeing my look of bewilderment, he adds, 'Now, I know you're not old enough to drink alcohol (I was still six months shy of my eighteenth birthday), but I'll buy you an orange juice. I don't suppose you've been in a pub before, have you?'

'No,' I lie, cringing inwardly, remembering how I'd sneaked off to The Grapes and got told off by a policeman during my St Michael's dance days, and all the other occasions I'd been in a pub since.

The Wheatsheaf, two minutes' walk away from the office, is an old-fashioned pub with low-beamed ceilings, chairs in jaded chintz, and a faded cream-and-brown carpet. It has a cosy atmosphere, smelling of roasted meats, cigars, and stale beer. But to my young senses, it also smells of a heady and thrilling decadence; suddenly I feel as if I've entered a grown-up world as a bona fide member, not as some kid metaphorically sneaking in through the back door.

Though I'm not aware of this at the time, The Wheatsheaf will eventually become a sort of second home to me, along with several other local hostelries, as I become acquainted with two of the cardinal rules of journalism: firstly, the pub serves as a hotbed of information and therefore a valuable source of 'news.' And secondly, and perhaps more importantly, it offers vital respite for overworked newspaper staff.

It's all a world away from the newspapers of today, where

staff are likely to be too time-pressured to even have a lunch break let alone adjourn to the pub, wolfing down sandwiches as they bash out stories on their keypads in their battle to meet deadlines. During the seventies we worked hard – but we played even harder, as I'm soon to discover.

As I sip my Britvic orange juice and Tom his pint of Yorkshire bitter, I learn a bit more about what he expects from me as a worker, and gain a glimpse into his somewhat unconventional management style.

'I'm not like any other boss,' he tells me in his broad Yorkshire brogue, ash flying all over the table from his cigar. 'And this isn't like any other newspaper. I'm not going to be standing over you, breathing down your neck, like they do on other papers, telling you what to do all the time. I want you to develop your own work and your own ideas. Because we have such a small staff at *The Courier*,' he continues, 'you'll get far better training than you would on the bigger papers – courts, council meetings, local events, police calls, fire calls, you'll cover the lot.'

Tantalisingly, he adds, 'We don't work regular hours here, so it's up to you what hours you work. If you want to finish at three o'clock on a Wednesday afternoon, when the pages are finished, then that's up to you. If you don't want to come in on Thursdays, when the paper is printed, then that's up to you, too. The most important thing is that we bring a paper out every week. And fill it with stories of people.'

Within this last revealing sentence, I quickly grasp the subtext behind his laissez-faire approach. During the interview I'd already learnt that I would be expected to work during the evenings, covering council meetings. There would also be weekend work, attending agricultural shows, garden parties, fetes and the like. It doesn't take me long to work out that behind Tom's magnanimity there lurks a cunning approach to extracting the maximum from his staff. And, as my career progresses, this is exactly what he gets from me. For, even at such a tender age,

I find myself relishing the freedom, flexibility, responsibility and sense of purpose my job gives me, not to mention the sense of trust that he bestows upon me. And it's fair to say that, as a result, I probably put far more in to my work than would be expected for a junior reporter.

Tom was certainly the most unorthodox boss I've ever had. Bohemian by character, he lived by his own rules, often not arriving at his desk until mid-morning, before coolly sauntering off home for an extended lunch at 1 p.m. and not returning to the office until late afternoon. On Tuesday evenings, he would work late into the night to catch up on lost hours as Wednesday's deadline approached. He dressed scruffily, in brown leather coat with brown woolly scarf, beige-and-brown checked serge shirt, cream trousers held up by thick braces, his red hair straggly and unkempt, puffing away at his obligatory cigar.

He was a curious mix of hard-drinking, hard-bitten journo, worn weary with cynicism from years of grafting on national newspapers, yet he was a sensitive soul, with a love of nature, art and beauty. He had an outrageous and irreverent sense of humour and would laugh uproariously at his own jokes, nearly choking on his cigar as he did so. Yet above all this, he was a fatherly figure, always ready to offer encouragement and keen to nurture new staff. I don't recall him ever raising his voice to me in all the years we worked together.

As we leave The Wheatsheaf on that first day, Tom makes another surprise announcement. 'Well, Angela,' he says to me, 'You've had your first day at *The Courier*. I want you to go home and think about everything I've told you and come back tomorrow, bright and early, ready to start your work.'

It's one o'clock in the afternoon – and I've barely completed a half-day at work! Feeling somewhat reluctant, like a child who has been ordered to leave a birthday party before the candles have been blown out on the cake, I catch the early afternoon bus back to Pilling. Arriving home, as I walk past our kitchen window to reach the back door, my mum's face is a picture: there's no mistaking the look of frozen horror.

'What's happened?' she shrieks as I enter the kitchen. From her expression, I know exactly what she's thinking. She thinks I've walked out on my first day. Or, worse, been ordered out.

I tell her what happened and her relief is palpable. It's only now, years later, that I reflect on the real reason for Tom's sending me home early: I suspect it has less to do with being a charitable gesture on his part and more to do with him having got behind with his work and needing to put a spurt on in order to meet Wednesday's deadline for 'putting the paper to bed' – ready to go to print the next day. Having to be bothered with a very raw junior reporter was probably the last thing he would have wanted that May afternoon.

There is one more surprise for me as I open the next week's edition of *The Garstang Courier*. Lurking in the bottom left-hand corner of the front page, is a head and shoulders photograph of me, under the headline, 'ANGELA JOINS THE COURIER'.

Underneath is a two-paragraph story which reads: 'Angela France, aged seventeen, from Pilling, has joined *The Courier* as a junior reporter. Angela will be out and about looking for stories. To tell her your news, contact her on …'

So here I am, my name in print. It's official: I'm *The Courier*'s new junior reporter! And the whole world knows about it. Or, at least, the world inhabited by *The Courier*'s five thousand-strong circulation footprint. All it needs now is for me to master that Olivetti …

35

'On the Road Again'

My first ever assignment as a junior reporter can hardly be described as headline-grabbing news. I'm dispatched to a children's summer fete and sports day in the tiny village of Abbeystead, nestling in the beautiful Bowland Fells. My task is to interview the organisers, observe the action and gather enough information to write a short report describing the day, to accompany the photos.

What makes this memorable is that it's my first trip with *The Courier*'s taciturn photographer, Johnny Smart, driving in his blue Ford Cortina. If Johnny ever wanted a career change he might have considered rally driving, for there's no doubt about it, he's a speed king, careering along the twisting, winding lanes at 70 mph as I cling to the sides of the seat, snapping my eyes closed each time we approach a right-hand bend on the wrong side of the road, tyres screeching, like something out of *Starsky and Hutch*. I try to distract him with conversation, in the hope of getting him to slow down, but to no avail.

'Do you like driving?' I inquire pleasantly.

'Hmmph,' is his monosyllabic response.

'How long have you been at *The Courier*?'

'Three years,' he grunts, eyes fixed ahead, hands glued to his steering wheel. I realise that making idle conversation isn't one of his strongest points.

If Johnny is a fast driver, he's an even speedier photographer.

His poor subjects rarely have time to compose themselves before he starts snapping away. A click with his camera here, another click there: job finished, no messing. That's his fast and furious philosophy; yet it seems to work, for his photos are nearly always surprisingly good at capturing the spontaneity of the moment.

The children's fete is on a field fringed by gorse bushes in gorgeous yellow bloom, flanked by the fells. It's packed with excited children and their watching parents. Johnny marshals a group of children in to a neat row, urges them to look his way, then snaps on his camera as quickly as you can say 'egg-and-spoon race.' A few action shots of kids running in the sack race and he's finished, camera packed up, ready to depart.

I, in the meantime, am busy trying to scribble notes. Primed by Tom to ask as many questions as possible, I subject the poor organisers of the field day to what must seem like an interminable interrogation: how long has this event been going on? How many people are involved? How much money is raised? How much do they charge people to enter the races (a daft question, considering these are races for children and likely to be free)? How do they think the day has gone? What time did it start? What time does it finish? Will there be anything else like it next year? And so on … and on …

The lady at the wooden bench, who is busy trying to answer my questions at the same time as recording the winners of the egg-and-spoon race, as well as seeking to console a sad-eyed little boy who came last because he kept dropping his 'wobbly egg', is beginning to look perplexed. Johnny, standing close by, camera slung over his shoulder, is glaring at me crossly. I read his hint, give my thanks and go.

Back at the office, I start to write my report. By now, the Olivetti and I are becoming better acquainted (though the wastepaper bin is still greatly in use); its keys are yielding to my touch, and I find I can create real words and even sentences, rather than the incomprehensible jibberish that confronted me on my first day. They are not, alas, always the right words and sentences for a newspaper, as I discover when Tom checks my copy.

My story reads something like this:

On Saturday 7 May, the school at Abbeystead organised a fete and field day for the children which was to raise funds for the school. It was a lovely sunny day and over 100 children from Abbeystead primary school took part in races, which started at 1.30 p.m. and finished at 4.30 p.m. There was an egg-and-spoon race, sack race and wheelbarrow race. There was also a sack race for the fathers, which was won by Jim Johnson, who lives at Deepdale Farm. As well as the races, there were lots of stalls, including an ice-cream stall, donkey rides and a miniature fairground. The sum raised was £400 and the money will be spent on school funds.

'Not bad,' says Tom, before launching in to his critique. Apparently, I've answered the Where? Who? What? When? and Why? questions, fundamental to any journalistic enquiry. These are crucial questions covering things such as where the event takes place, who is involved, what is happening, and why it is happening. But by starting with the date, I've already made the story sound like old news and it will look dated by the time it appears in the paper. I've also included information that readers won't be interested in, such as start and finish times.

Tom rewrites my story and it reads very differently:

The sun shone down on Abbeystead's children's fete and sports day, when more than 100 children and their parents enjoyed an afternoon of sports and fun. Youngsters from Abbeystead Primary School took part in a variety of races, including the egg-and-spoon and wheelbarrow race. There was even a sack race for the dads, won by farmer Jim Johnson. The ice-cream stall, donkey rides and miniature fairground all did a roaring trade and the event raised £400 towards school funds.

I'm beginning to learn how to write as a journalist.

'Keep your sentences short, concise and punchy,' Tom counsels. 'Imagine your *Courier* reader is someone who wants to pick up the paper over a cup of tea and a biscuit. They don't want to be bothered with fancy, flowery words and sentences they don't understand. They just want information that makes sense to them.'

That Friday, Tom has included the rewritten version of my story in the paper as part of a double-page spread on Abbeystead field day and children's fete. In the midst of half a dozen or so photographs of children gleefully competing in the egg-and-spoon and sack races ('pictures with children in them sell papers') is my story. Above the text are the words: 'Photographs by Johnny Smart. Words by Angela France.' My first ever newspaper byline!

Over the coming weeks, I'm dispatched to shadow Jack Dooley, the paper's chief reporter and Tom's son, while he covers police and fire calls. Jack is a couple of years older than me. He's the polar opposite of Tom: where Tom is gregarious, Jack is shy, diffident and socially awkward, yet wears the supercilious air of one who knows he is the boss's son and therefore beyond reproach. Like Johnny Smart, he's a master of the monosyllable. He is tall, but walks with an ungainly stooped posture, taking big lolloping strides.

Garstang police station is perched atop a small hill in Garstang's Bowgreave area, and is headed by a belligerent, rotund inspector, with a staff of three sergeants and several constables. Police calls are, Jack informs me, an important part of the work of a journalist, because it is through these that we get to hear of any crime – usually burglaries – or any accidents or incidents that might have happened. By becoming habitual visitors and telephone callers to the police station, we're on the ball if any major news stories break out.

For my first visit, I'm there to observe as Jack asks the thin-faced Scots sergeant on the enquiry desk if there is anything newsworthy. The officer flicks through his thick leather-bound file, sifting through the pink incident sheets (this was in the days before incidents were logged on to a computer).

'There was a burglary at a farm at St Michael's, Saturday night,' he reports. 'Two power drills and a child's bicycle.'

It's hardly headline news, but Jack tells me it will make a useful single paragraph NIB – news in brief – filler item for the paper. NIBs serve a vital purpose: they help to fill gaps in the page. Not only that, but they provide interesting snippets of information and add variety and visual appeal to the page.

Jack scribbles the detail in shorthand in his notebook, slips the book in his pocket, utters a curt 'thank you' and we're off. That's it: little more than a brief, terse exchange of information, lasting a matter of minutes. It isn't until my formal training, many months later, that I become aware that Jack has overlooked one of the central tenets of the journalist's role: that of relationship building; for it is only by getting to know our contacts and building an effective working relationship with them that trust can develop. Who knows what else that Scots sergeant might have told us that day that might have been useful to us, had we chosen to linger that morning, passing time with a bit of gentle conversation and banter? He might have proffered some insider information on a covert surveillance operation for all we knew …

It was a similar story when I accompanied Jack to see the chief fire officer. Back then, Garstang was, and still is, covered by a retained fire service; part-time fire officers who live in the community and are on standby in the event of an emergency.

The fire team leader combines his role with running a family hardware business at his shop in the centre of Garstang. We call in just as he has finished serving a customer.

'Have you anything for us?' Jack asks hopefully, notebook poised. The fire chief screws up his face, trying to summon his powers of recall (there's no incident book here).

'A chimney fire in Garstang on Monday,' he says. 'Oh, and a cow stuck in a ditch in Winmarleigh yesterday.' Jack scribbles down the details and we depart.

After a week or two, I'm allowed out on my own, entrusted to build up, cultivate and nurture my own network of contacts who will feed me with all-important news. Over time, I get to know all the officers at Garstang police station on first-name terms and enjoy having banter with them.

Unlike today's hard-pressed journos who seldom seem to get out of the office, we were fortunate enough to have the luxury of time to have a cup of tea and a chat with our contacts. It was part of the relationship-building and trust that was all-important on a local newspaper like ours.

I learn how to develop a 'nose' for news, beginning to distinguish between legitimate news and potentially libellous slander, though there is seldom anything even remotely salacious. In our cosy rural world, a head teacher retiring, a vicar winning a prize for growing the best dahlias, or a councillor being caught stealing milk all count as news, though hardly of the earth-shattering variety.

Fulfilling a promise made to Tom at my interview, I start driving lessons.

On some days my boss would treat me to an impromptu driving lesson, allowing me to drive his blue Mini Clubman – which, for some strange reason, he christened his 'ice-cream van' – while he sat next to me in the passenger seat, nervously barking his instructions.

There is one particular occasion that never fails to make me smile as I remember it. We are driving to *The Courier*'s head office in Morecambe, where the paper is printed, one Thursday morning, to give me the chance to observe the printing process. I am at the wheel and he is in the passenger seat. As we approach a set of traffic lights on the main road in to Morecambe, I judge – correctly as it happens – that I have enough time to make it through the lights before they change from green to amber. Tom, alas, has less faith. Without warning he raises his knees and plants both feet firmly on the faux polished walnut dashboard in front of him, keeping them there for the remainder of our journey. It hardly inspires confidence in my ability as a driver. I don't think he volunteered to take me out driving after that.

After three attempts, I pass my driving test. Soon I am the proud owner of my first car: a nippy, dinky little Mini in navy blue, bought from an acquaintance of my family for £90.

My new car opens up a whole world for me, at work and socially. It means that in my job I can broaden my network of contacts, zipping along the country lanes to the outlying villages to call on vicars, police officers, councillors, fire officers, shopkeepers, Women's Institute groups, amateur dramatic societies and anyone else who might help me in my never-ending quest to find stories to fill the next week's *Courier*.

One morning, I'm driving along a leafy lane after visiting a headteacher at a primary school in Calder Vale, a pretty mill village nestling in a dip, hugged by the Bowland Fells. It's a beautiful day and the trees and fields are lush with the verdant greens of summer. Judy Collins' hauntingly melodic 'Send in the Clowns' is ringing out from the car radio. As the radiance from that summer's day seeps into every pore of my skin, I'm struck by a sudden realisation of my good fortune: here I am, doing a job I love and actually getting paid for it.

After about three months in my role, Tom calls me into his office. I have successfully completed my probationary period, he tells me, and he would like to take me on as an indentured journalist. This is a legal contract with Lancaster and Morecambe Newspapers, parent company of *The Courier*, which means they will take responsibility for training me to become a fully qualified journalist. In turn, I will have to agree to serve my time and to attend a training course on one day each week. Tom explains that my training will take place at an independent printing college in Liverpool.

'What do you think?' he says.

What do I think? I'm ecstatic! It means I'm one step nearer towards my dream of becoming a fully fledged journalist. What would Mr Gledhill, the teacher at St Aidan's who was so dismissive of my aspirations, think of me now?

36

'Everlasting Love'

So what happened to that shy blond-haired boy from Manchester who started Pilling CE School on the same day as me and whose story ran parallel to my own? Though we lived in the same village and were in the same year group at St Aidan's School, and although we went to confirmation classes and to Preesall youth club at the same time, Keith Norris and I didn't really know each other. He was just some boy who seemed to hover around in the background of my life; I doubt whether we'd spoken more than half a dozen words in all those years. Football was central to his world, just as dancing and fashion were mine.

Things changed the day I went knocking on the door of Pilling police station, where PC Ted Norris was the bobby, in search of news. He turned out to be one of my most reliable contacts. Back then, each village had its own police house, occupied by the resident local copper and his or her family, identifiable by its distinctive blue door and exterior white globe-shaped light, with 'Police' emblazoned across it in black letters.

Pilling police station happened to be the family home of PC Norris and his large brood. The first time I knocked on the imposing front door, it was PC Norris's shy, blond-haired son who opened it. Intuitively, I knew he was eyeing me up and down. The feeling was mutual; there was a definite frisson. Here he was, with a thatch of thick, blond hair worn to his collar bone, a loose floppy fringe, warm grey-blue eyes that crinkled when he smiled, and a soft, gentle mouth. Why had I never noticed him before?

It was to be several weeks before shy Keith Norris, by now working as an apprentice electrician, plucked up the courage to ask me out. The occasion was St Michael's dance. I like to think God must have been in a good mood that night, intent on playing celestial cupid to our romance, because it was only by sheer chance that we both happened to be there. Each of us arrived at the dance hall separately. And we were on our own.

That particular evening, for some reason, most of my friends had cried off the dance. But at the last minute I decided to make an effort and go anyway, fully expecting there would be lots of people I knew. I took myself off to the dance hall, about seven miles away, in my little blue Mini.

In the meantime, Keith had been playing football that afternoon; he played for Pilling FC in the North Lancashire League. When he got home, it was too late to arrange a rendezvous with his friends. Anticipating they would be going to St Michael's, he decided to make his own way there, only to find none of his friends had turned up.

So here we are, Keith Norris and I, both on our own, yet somehow managing to merge ourselves into the same crowd of mutual acquaintances, each of us striving to look nonchalant, yet each seeming to be connected by a sizzling undercurrent of electric fire infused with anticipation. I find some girls to dance with. Status Quo's 'Rocking All Over the World' is blasting out across the room; cue some pretty frenetic dancing: hands on hips, bending torso from the waist, dipping alternate elbows towards the floor, aping the macho dance style adopted by those male rockers at Stalmine disco what seems like light years ago. It's hardly an appropriate choice for a romantic build-up.

Seconds later, 'Tiger Feet' by upcoming glam-rockers Mud reverberates across the dance hall. I love its catchy rhythm, and the flamboyant eccentric dance craze that accompanies it. You step forward with your left foot, swing your right leg over in a sort of exaggerated semicircle, while at the same time stepping back with your left foot. The whole sequence is repeated over and again as you move in stylish rotations, hips swaying, legs swinging, in time to the beat. When done in sync with other dancers, creating a rhythmic flow, this relatively simple dance can look pretty impressive. And there is nothing more important to me at that moment than making an impression on this shy seventeen-year-old boy.

Inwardly, I will him to ask me to go out with him. 'Just Do it, Now! Please!' I steal sideways glances as he stands coolly in one corner of the room, hands in pockets, handsome in his green checked Ben Sherman shirt and blue jeans. Instinct tells me he is taking surreptitious glances at me beneath his lowered eyes.

At midnight, the dancing finishes and the lights come on. The DJ is still on the stage, clearing away his paraphernalia. A crowd of a dozen or so congregates in the middle of the dance floor, Keith Norris among them. They're just hanging around talking. I sidle across to them. Inwardly, I rehearse ways of striking up a conversation with him, asking him if he fancies going to the pictures. In the chauvinistic seventies, it is still the prerogative of the boy to ask the girl out. By altering the rules, I risk appearing brazen and foolhardy, not to mention the burning agony of rejection.

Out of the corner of my eye, I notice Keith has shuffled next to me. There's a trapeze artist in my tummy as he starts talking to me. He is speaking in a barely audible voice, eyes averted to the floor. I can't remember what he says exactly, and nor can he. But I can remember how our conversation finishes: 'D'ya fancy coming out for a drink tomorrow night?' By now the trapeze artist is in full fury of movement as, flushing, I accept his invitation. I can't believe it. I've just bagged the date of my dreams!

The next evening he picks me up in his cherry-red Hillman

California. I dress demurely, wearing a navy blue velour cowl-necked jumper and matching navy skirt. We go to the Farmer's Arms in the village of Great Eccleston, about six miles away.

Unbeknown to me, he's also invited his younger sister Patsy and her boyfriend for moral support. They are waiting at the pub when we get there.

As first dates go, it's a non-event. The pub is quiet, devoid of customers on a chill November evening. Keith looks gorgeous in a black jumper. As we settle in the lounge bar, we make idle chit-chat but it's Patsy's garrulous boyfriend who keeps the conversation flowing. A couple of half-lagers later and we're on our way home. As he drops me off outside our house, Keith leans over to give me a swift, tentative peck on the cheek and asks me if I fancy going to the pictures the following week.

So that was it: my first date. Mulling everything over in my head that night as I await sleep, I can't help but feel a sense of anticlimax; where were those bright flames of romance I'd so longed for?

If my first date with Keith was unmemorable, my second date was certainly different – but for all the wrong reasons.

'How do you fancy going to see *Stardust*?' he asked me as I stepped inside his Hillman. *Stardust*, featuring adorable, tousled-haired David Essex and Adam Faith, was the sequel to *That'll Be the Day*, the film set in the fifties rock 'n' roll era. Of course I wanted to go; who wouldn't?

We drive to the ABC Princess in Blackpool, where we meet Patsy and her boyfriend. Inside the auditorium, it's busy; we opt for middle-row seats, settling in to the plush red velvet chairs. The curtain rises and the celluloid screen fills with images – but they're not the sort we are expecting from *Stardust*. Bare-breasted women and bare-bottomed men flaunt their bodies across the screen and there's a lot of saucy language from the lecherous male lead. At first, we assume this is a trailer for another film. But, no: twenty minutes later things are getting raunchier by the minute, and still no David Essex in sight. It turns out that we've paid to see a sex film!

Instead of *Stardust*, we're watching *Keep it Up, Jack*, a dubious comedy sex romp about a failed music-hall performer who inherits a brothel when his aunt dies. He takes over the running of the business and falls in love with a beautiful prostitute. It's full of innuendo characteristic of seventies film and television, epitomised by the likes of Benny Hill, with added nudity.

'I'm so sorry', says poor Keith over and over, plainly embarrassed by his gaff. I tell him not to worry and later we laugh it off. In some ways, it probably helps to break down the wall of shyness that existed between us. Years later, we still laugh about the night he took me to a sex film on our second date.

After that we settled in to a routine of going to the pub. Keith disliked dancing so we stopped going to dances and ended up going out for a drink instead, becoming intimately acquainted with all the pubs and hostelries in rural Over Wyre. Within a few weeks of our getting together, Keith swapped his Hillman for a maroon Vauxhall Viva, and against the soundtrack of 10cc, the Beatles and The Moody Blues blasting out from his car stereo as we meandered along the winding country lanes, the tender shoots of our romance blossomed into a great big fruit tree, sun-ripened with love.

A few months later, we cemented our relationship with a week away in Torquay. Checking in to our hotel, a jaded former Victorian mansion, peopled by geriatric guests, I can remember the illicit thrill when we were shown up to our tiny attic room, housed in what was probably the servants' quarters back in its illustrious days. Even in 1975, despite increasing sexual liberation offered by the contraceptive pill, there was still a strong sense of moral propriety around, which meant behaving covertly and with sensitivity to others. The hotel owners knew we weren't married and their decamping of us to an attic bedroom seemed a none-too-subtle ploy to ensure we remained discretely out of view of the other elderly guests. But it was that clandestine element that made it all seem so much more exciting.

The hotel owner was a tall bespectacled man with a mane of fiery red hair, swept back. He went by the unfortunate name of Mr Crump – and he looked alarmingly like Mr Shelley! We spent the week in fits of giggles, imagining our erstwhile head teacher had come to haunt us, and to spy on our nights of passion.

I loved Keith's laid-back quality, his down-to-earth personality, his dependability. Beneath his shy exterior, there lurked a sharp sense of humour and a warm, easy wit. Like me, he had a strong work ethic, motivated by a desire to succeed, and we shared the same interests in music and the outdoors. As well as all this, my parents approved of him, and it didn't seem long before my mum spotted 'husband' potential.

'Don't let him go,' she cautioned. 'You'll never get another like him.' It was the best bit of advice she'd ever given to me. And yes, many years later, you've probably guessed what happened to that shy, blond-haired boy I started primary school with all those years ago: reader, I married him!

Afterword

Keith Norris and I were married on Easter Saturday, 25 March 1978, a cold day driven by strong winds and snow showers. We were both just twenty-one years old, ludicrously young by today's standards, yet probably no different than many of our contemporaries back then. After honeymooning for three days at a Keswick guesthouse, we couldn't wait to get back to our first house, a neat three-bedroomed semi on the outskirts of Garstang, chosen for its proximity to my job at *The Courier* and Keith's job as an electrician with a Garstang firm.

Eighteen months later, our first child Gavin was born. We moved to Preesall to be nearer family. I went back to work part-time, leaving my baby in the care of his doting grandparents. In February 1982, Tom Dooley called me in to his office and told me to close the door behind me.

'I'm leaving *The Courier*,' he declared wearily. He didn't have a job to go to, but I knew he had a lucrative sideline writing short stories for women's magazines under a female pseudonym (though he never spoke openly of this). He was guarded about his plans, as he was about much of his private life. But I sensed he just wanted out from the relentless pressure of producing a newspaper week in, week out.

Tom's decision was the catalyst for me to make a life-changing decision of my own: I'd already felt I was missing out on bringing my baby up by working part-time. In discussion with Keith, I decided to hand my notice in and focus on motherhood. Back in the seventies it was still very much the norm to be a stay-at-home mum. Leaving *The Courier* meant we were much poorer, yet somehow we managed to scrape by, even though it meant foregoing many luxuries, and living in handed-down clothes.

On New Year's Day 1983 I made my own 'news' when our second son Darren was born – one of a handful of New Year babies to be feted by the local papers. Our picture was plastered on the front page of *The Courier*. Immersed as I was in motherhood, I still found time to write for *The Courier* on a freelance basis for many years while the children were young. Later, I got a part-time job as a reporter on *The Lancaster and Morecambe Citizen*.

Reaching my mid-thirties, I was restless, ready for a career change. Fed up with chasing fire engines, I felt I wanted to do something more worthwhile and of benefit to other people. I'd always been interested in health, having enjoyed Miss Bennett's health education classes while at school, and it was this that propelled me to become a mature student studying for a degree in health promotion studies. After graduating in 1995, I got a job in the NHS working as a health promotion specialist, supporting schools to tackle issues such as drugs, alcohol and sex education.

After the NHS, I did a little bit of lecturing and research. In 2009, I joined a health watchdog organisation as a community engagement officer. My job included gathering people's stories about their experiences of health services. It was a role I loved, mainly because it felt like I was heading back towards my journalistic roots. My last employment, as the manager of a lovely project organising arts workshops and cinema screenings for people with dementia, drew to a close when the funding ran out. It seemed the right time to draw the curtains on my career.

Since finishing work, I've returned to my first love: writing. As well as my own life story, I've written short life stories and tributes for other people. Keith Norris and I are still together, more than forty years after we met as gauche teenagers at St Michael's dance, undoubtedly greyer, but hopefully a little wiser …

My life story began in Knott End, and I'm still here,

enjoying my semi-retirement years watching the lapping waves of the tide ebbing and flowing ceaselessly, their many moods – stormy and tempestuous one day, serene and benign the next – reflecting life itself and all its highs and lows, its shades of light and dark.

Acknowledgements

I am indebted to the many people who have helped me in writing this story. Particular thanks must go to Don Stringfellow for providing me with useful background information on Knott End and Preesall in the sixties, and on the history of Knott End as a holiday resort. I am also grateful to those who shared their recollections of this era: Raymond Fenton, Rosemary Hogarth, Pat Kershaw, Bob Croft, Marion Williamson, my dad Roy France, my aunts June Storey and Peggy Carter, Peter and Judith Atkinson and Colin Cross.

Thanks must also go also to my mum's cousin, Pat, for providing missing elements of my family history, to my former teachers, Christine Bennett, George Maund and David Evans, for filling in memory gaps relating to my time at St Aidan's, and to Graham Curwen, Liz Ainsworth, John Higginson, and Mick and John Piela for sharing their memories of youth club and dances.

Among my many former school friends, I'd like to thank Anne Bell (nee Rossall), Gill Raby, Lynn and Anne Bleasdale, Janice Cookson, Vivien Cornall, Lynn Henderson and Enid Cross, for their kind support. Thanks must also go to author Edward Campbell, who very kindly read through my story during its very early drafts and passed on his wisdom and warmth.

Finally, I would like to thank Keith Norris, that one-time shy blond-haired boy, for his unstinting support and love, and without whom there would have been no story.

Eleven-plus test papers, answers:

Test One

1. Quiz, quite flux,flute plan, *plate*
2. Practice, price stopping, sting pleasant, *plant*
3. Pat, pout flat,flout rat, *rout*
4. Sludge, slug fudge, fug budge,*bug*
5. Frame,blame fright,blight frown, *flown*

Test Two

1. Who does French but does not do art? *Fern*
2. Who does chemistry but not geography? *Naomi*
3. Who does art and Spanish but does not do geography and textiles? *Husna*
4. Who does not study music, Greek or Spanish? *Deborah*
5. Who does the fewest subjects? *Naomi*